SANDEEP CHATTER[...]

QUICK & EA[...]

INDIAN

VEGETARIAN COOKERY

SANDEEP CHATTERJEE'S
QUICK & EASY
INDIAN
VEGETARIAN COOKERY

BBC BOOKS

To my parents, Ma and Babai

Published by BBC Books,
a division of BBC Enterprises Limited
Woodlands, 80 Wood Lane, London W12 0TT

First published 1992
© Sandeep Chatterjee 1992
The moral right of the author has been asserted
ISBN 0 563 36325 8

Designed by Peter Bridgewater
Illustrations by Lorraine Harrison
Photographs by George Seper
Styling by Janice Baker
Photoset in Bembo by Redwood Press, Melksham, Wiltshire
Printed and bound in Great Britain by Clays Ltd, St Ives plc
Colour separations by Technik Ltd
Cover printed by Clays Ltd, St Ives plc

ACKNOWLEDGEMENTS

I wish to express my gratitude to everyone who has helped me with the preparation of this book, especially my wife Sita without whose assistance it would not have been possible. My thanks also to Jane Adams for her valuable support and comments.

I would also like to acknowledge the Taj Group of Hotels, particularly Mr Ajit Kerkar, Ms Camilia Punjabi and Mr Subhir Bowmick with whom it all started. And finally, many thanks to everyone at the Bombay Heritage and Best of Bombay, especially Mr Tirandaz Kermani.

BBC BOOKS
QUICK AND EASY COOKERY SERIES

Launched in 1989 by Ken Hom and Sarah Brown, the *Quick and Easy Cookery* series is a culinary winner. Everything about the titles is aimed at quick and easy recipes – the store-cupboard introductions, the ingredients and cooking methods, the menu section at the back of the books. Eight pages of colour photographs are also included to provide a flash of inspiration for the frantic or faint-hearted.

Other titles in the series:

Ken Hom's Quick and Easy Chinese Cookery
Sarah Brown's Quick and Easy Vegetarian Cookery
Clare Connery's Quick and Easy Salads
Joanna Farrow's Quick and Easy Fish Cookery
Beverley Piper's Quick and Easy Healthy Cookery
All at £5.99.

CONTENTS

INTRODUCTION

In recent years more and more people have been deciding to become vegetarian. With its emphasis on using a variety of vegetables flavoured with interesting and subtle spices, Indian cuisine offers a totally balanced and delicious vegetarian alternative.

An Indian cook is rather like an artist who uses varied spices from his painter's palette to colour and flavour food. Each time you add or take out a spice or even change its form (by using it, say, whole, crushed or powdered), you create a new dish. This is perhaps the greatest beauty of Indian cooking. There are no rigid ways of making a dish. It is an art form – the common man's appreciation of nature's bounty.

However, there are a number of myths about Indian cooking which this book aims to dispel. The most common misconception is that Asian cuisine is very laborious and time-consuming. But these days most ordinary kitchens contain equipment which can keep preparation time down to a matter of minutes. By using a coffee grinder, for instance, one can drastically reduce the time spent on grinding spices.

I have used all the recipes in this book over the years and the time taken to cook them has been continuously reduced. This is not only due to better equipment; it is also because the quality of ready-prepared food has vastly improved. Whereas some time ago it would take 15–20 minutes to extract coconut milk, now one just has to open a tin. Though lots of frozen vegetables are available in the shops, I would generally recommend only fresh vegetables for cooking as they remain much crunchier and tastier. However, high-quality frozen peas are certainly a good substitute for fresh ones.

Having your spices handy while cooking also cuts down on preparation time. I usually have the most common spices in small jars and put them all on a tray which can easily be moved around wherever needed.

Another oft-repeated myth is that Indian food is always hot. It is true that this cuisine is spicy but the heat is entirely optional. You will find that many of my recipes include up to 1 tablespoon of chilli powder. If, as I do, you enjoy hot food this is not an excessive measure. However if you prefer milder flavours a teaspoon may be a better quantity – at least until you establish your tolerance!

Also, if you find that you don't have one or two minor ingredients for a particular recipe you can always substitute something else or omit them altogether. As you become familiar with these recipes you will find that you can use them as a guide and create your own variations.

Once you have stocked your pantry, the cooking itself is usually very easy. The preparation times given assume that you will use the quickest and easiest methods, such as buying tinned chickpeas rather than soaking and cooking dried ones. Likewise, I have assumed that wherever possible you will put fresh spices in a food processor rather than chopping them by hand.

Finally, it's worth mentioning that most of the dishes can be prepared in advance and just heated through when serving. This makes Indian food very convenient both for entertaining and everyday meals, and many of the flavours actually improve with re-heating.

Notes on the Recipes

All recipes in this book serve four.
Follow one set of measurements only; do not mix metric and Imperial.
Eggs are size 2.
Spoon measurements are level.
Wash fresh produce before preparation.
Adjust strongly flavoured ingredients to suit your own taste.

COOKING EQUIPMENT

It is quite possible to cook Indian food in a sparsely equipped kitchen but a few Western and typically Indian utensils can be a great help.

KARAI/INDIAN WOK

The *karai* or Indian wok is usually made of cast iron, aluminium or brass. It is a very practical utensil which can be used for deep-frying (for which it uses much less oil than a deep-fat fryer). Because it is much thicker than a Chinese wok one can use it to cook food thoroughly, especially vegetables. If you cook Indian food quite often it is worth investing in one, but you can substitute a thickish wok or a deep non-stick frying pan.

TAVA

This is a round iron griddle plate which retains heat and distributes it evenly. It is used to make *rotis*, *parathas* and other Indian breads. If you are buying a *tava*, choose one which is heavy and fairly thick, with a handle. A thick cast iron pan can be used instead.

BLENDER/LIQUIDISER

This is essential for quick Indian cookery. Choose a blender with blades near the base as this enables one to blend small quantities. Many recipes begin with an instruction to blend fresh spices and water to make a paste. If you don't have a blender you can use a mortar and pestle, but you will need to allow extra time.

FOOD PROCESSOR

This can save a great deal of time that would otherwise be spent chopping ginger, chillies, garlic and other fresh spices. Again, if you don't have a food processor, you can do the chopping by hand, but you will need to allow extra time.

COFFEE GRINDER

This is another piece of equipment you really cannot do without. It is used to grind all the dry spices, particularly cumin and cardamom seeds.

SPATULA

A good spatula is another essential. A wooden one will do, but a metal one is better (unless you're using non-stick pans in which case plastic implements are preferable). Choose a spatula with an insulated handle.

PRESSURE COOKER

A pressure cooker is very useful, especially when cooking *dals* or boiling potatoes. It reduces the cooking time dramatically.

SPICE BOX

A spice box (or *masala dibba*) is very handy when cooking Indian food. It is a round steel container with a number of small containers in it, and a tight-fitting lid. You can put the most common spices in the containers so that you have them easily available when cooking. Indian spice shops usually sell these boxes. However they are by no means essential and can easily be replaced by small jars on a tray.

BASIC INDIAN PANTRY

Quick and easy cooking is really quick and easy once you have organised your pantry. You may need to go to Indian shops for some of the unusual items, but most of the ingredients you need are easily available in supermarkets and grocery shops.

In ideal circumstances, I would recommend buying spices whole and grinding them yourself in small quantities, but this is not always possible. Buy only small packets of spices because they tend to lose their fragrance and flavour over time. They should be stored in a dry place in air-tight containers, and commonly used spice mixtures (page 17) can be made up and stored in air-tight containers with a label.

Remember, the key to Indian vegetarian cooking is the freshness of the spices and the way they are combined and prepared.

AJWAIN

These small oval reddish or greenish-brown seeds have a strong flavour and the aroma of thyme. Used in deep-fried savoury dishes and as a stuffing for *parathas*, *ajwain* seeds are available whole or crushed from Asian food shops.

AMCHUR

Amchur is the dried unripe fruit of the Indian mango tree. When dried, the sliced mango turns dark brown and may be powdered. It is sour-sweet with a resinous bouquet, and can be used in curries, chutneys and marinades for fish or vegetables. *Amchur* is available from good Indian and Asian grocers in sliced or powdered form.

ASAFOETIDA

This spice is derived from the sap of the giant fennel, a member of the parsley family. The spice looks like reddish-brown crystals and is available in crystalline or powder form from Indian food shops. Normally used in minute quantities, it is a great flavour enhancer.

BAY LEAF

The large dried leaves of the bay laurel tree have a strong flavour and are often used in biryanis, kormas and curries. They should be removed before serving.

BLACK CUMIN SEEDS / KALA JEERA

These dark aromatic seeds are used in various vegetable dishes. They are only available from Asian grocers.

BLACK SALT

Black salt is available in granule or powder form from Asian food shops. It has a very pungent smell and goes well with yoghurt, but it is entirely optional in any recipe.

CARDAMOM

The cardamom bush is native to India and its seed pod is most commonly used whole. Three types of cardamom pod are available in the West – green, white and the larger black or brown cardamom. Green cardamom seeds are powdered and used in sweet and savoury dishes, but the brown seeds are more pungent and should only be used in savoury dishes.

Where the recipes in this book specify 'ground cardamom' you can use ready-ground cardamom for speed and convenience. However, for the best flavour, it is preferable to grind the seeds of green cardamom pods yourself, as required. If using whole cardamom pods in a dish, remove before serving.

CHANNA DAL

These round yellow lentils are usually only sold in Asian or Middle Eastern shops. Yellow split peas can be used as a substitute.

CHAT MASALA

This spice mixture is sold in packets in Asian spice shops. Keep in an air-tight container after opening.

CHICKPEA FLOUR / BESAN / GRAM FLOUR

Chickpea flour is usually only available in Asian food shops. Though it has a very distinctive flavour, you can substitute pea flour which can be found in health food shops. Alternatively, you could buy dried chickpeas, dry-roast them in a heavy-based pan and grind them in a coffee grinder.

CHILLIS

Chillies, both fresh and dried, are used all over India in many different forms, whether whole, slit, powdered or crushed. The intensity of heat varies with the method and amount used. Apart from giving the heat to Indian cuisine, chillies are also used as a colourful garnish. Chilli powder is available from supermarkets and Indian spice shops. It is often labelled 'mild', 'medium' or 'hot'. Choose the one best suited to your palate, and adjust the quantity you use to your taste.

If you wish to reduce the heat of fresh chillies you can de-seed them before chopping them or putting them in the food processor or blender.

One word of warning: remember not to touch your eyes or mouth while handling fresh chillies as they can cause irritation, and wash your hands as soon as possible afterwards.

CINNAMON

The cultivated dried bark of the cinnamon evergreen is sold in 'quills' (cinnamon sticks) or powdered. Whole pieces of cinnamon must be removed before serving.

CLOVES

The clove tree grows on the Malabar Coast and is a tropical evergreen. Cloves are actually the unopened flower buds which are dried to a dark brown. Sweet and pungent, with an irresistible aroma, cloves are used in *garam masala* spice mixture (page 17) and biryanis. Buy them whole and grind as necessary. Remove whole cloves before serving.

COCONUT

If you have the time, freshly grated coconut is delicious. However, many Asian shops now sell frozen grated coconut in packets. Alternatively, desiccated coconut is available from any supermarket and provides the ideal quick and easy substitute.

Coconut cream is available from many supermarkets in block form, and tinned coconut cream and coconut milk can be found in most Asian shops.

CORIANDER

The coriander plant is a member of the parsley family. Its aromatic leaves are often used as a garnish and the mild-flavoured ground seeds as a spice. Fresh coriander is available from Asian food shops and some supermarkets, and ground coriander is widely available.

CUMIN

Cumin seeds are small, boat-shaped, ridged and greenish-brown in colour. They have a strong aroma and flavour, and can be used both whole and powdered.

When the recipes in this book specify 'cumin seeds, roasted and ground', you should dry-roast the seeds in a frying pan until they turn dark brown, then grind them to a powder in a coffee grinder. Once made, the roasted cumin powder can be stored in an air-tight glass jar.

CURRY LEAVES

Curry leaves are shiny and evergreen, rather like small bay leaves. They are usually bruised and added to hot oil, and they have a sweet penetrating aroma. They can be bought either dried or semi-dried in some Indian and Asian shops.

FENNEL SEEDS

These seeds are curved, ridged and a dull yellow-green colour, rather like plumper and larger versions of anise seeds. They can always be found in Indian shops and are used in *panch phoran* spice mixture (page 18). Fennel seeds also go very well with spinach.

FENUGREEK

Both the leaves and seeds of fenugreek are used in Indian cuisine. The leaves are cooked as a vegetable and can be combined with potatoes. The seeds are an ochre-brown colour and resemble tiny pebbles. These are used both whole (for pickles) and powdered, and can be bought from Indian and Asian shops.

GARLIC

Fresh garlic is widely used, along with ginger, to give a rich aroma to curries. The longer garlic is cooked, the milder its flavour.

GHEE

Ghee is clarified butter and is very widely available in supermarkets and Asian shops. Ghee has a nice flavour and goes especially well with vegetables, but you could substitute any vegetable oil, groundnut oil, corn oil or sunflower oil.

GINGER

This pleasantly pungent rhizome is used in many forms. Fresh ginger is peeled, then ground to a paste, grated, chopped or crushed and used as a basic flavouring. It is available in Indian shops and many supermarkets, as is dried ground ginger.

KALONJI/NIGELLA SEEDS

These tiny, black, teardrop-shaped seeds are crunchy, bitter and peppery, with a faint nutmeg aroma. In Northern India they are sprinkled on top of *naans* before baking. They are also used in *panch phoran* spice mixture (page 18).

MACE

Mace is the dried, lacy, crimson outer covering of the nutmeg. It has a similar flavour to nutmeg but is much more pungent and should therefore be used with caution.

METHI

The dried leaves of the *methi* plant are used as a finishing spice. You can buy them in packets from some Asian shops.

MUNG BEANS/MOONG DAL

Whole mung beans are often sprouted for use in salads. To do this, soak the mung beans overnight in water then drain and leave at room temperature for 1–2 days until they sprout, rinsing with water occasionally. Sprouting containers are commonly available, but you could use any large glass jar or bowl and cover the top with muslin.

Whole mung beans are available in many health food shops and some supermarkets. Skinned and split mung beans (*moong dal*) can be found in most Asian food shops.

MUSTARD

Mustard is used all over India in many forms. The leaves are prepared as a vegetable; the seeds are ground to a paste or kept whole; and mustard oil (only available from Asian shops) is used in cooking. Whole brown mustard seeds, when popped in hot oil, lose their pungency and become sweet and nutty.

NUTMEG

The nutmeg kernel is dark brown and hard on the outside and paler inside. The flavour is similar to mace but milder. Buy nutmeg whole if you can and grate it directly over the dish. It is used in many masalas and goes well with spinach. Ready-ground and whole nutmegs are available in most supermarkets.

OKRA/LADIES FINGERS

This unusually shaped, pointed green vegetable is used in Indian, Mexican and Middle Eastern cuisine. Fresh okra is available from good greengrocers and some supermarkets. Canned okra can be found in some Asian shops, though it is preferable to use it fresh.

PEPPER

Pepper is native to Southern India and the berries ripen from green to reddish-yellow. Black peppercorns, the dried unripe corns of the pepper vine, and green pickled peppercorns are the ones used in Indian cooking. Where the variety is not specified, use crushed black peppercorns.

POPPY SEEDS

The opium poppy yields harmless and delicious poppy seeds which can be used in cooking. In India we use the creamy white ones which are available from Indian shops. They are ground to a paste and used in kormas, curries and other savoury dishes.

RICE FLOUR

Flour made from ground raw rice is used extensively in Southern India, often as a thickening or crisping agent. It is available from delicatessens or Asian shops.

RICE VERMICELLI

This is usually available from Indian shops and supermarkets.

ROSE WATER

This diluted essence of rose petals is mainly used in sweet drinks and desserts. Use sparingly for a subtle flavour. Rose water is available from some health food shops and Asian shops.

SAFFRON

Saffron, the dried stigma of the crocus flower, is the world's most expensive spice. It imparts a distinctive aroma, a bitter honey-like taste and a golden-yellow colour. It is used in rich biryanis, curries and desserts. For maximum colour and flavour, saffron threads can be soaked in hot milk for a few minutes before use.

SAGO

Sago can be found in supermarkets with the cake and pudding ingredients. It is usually soaked for about 30 minutes before use, in just enough water to cover.

SEMOLINA

This wheat product comes ready-packed and graded from fine to medium or coarse. It can be found in most supermarkets as well as Asian and Italian food shops.

SESAME SEEDS

Sesame, a tropical annual, bears small, flat oval seeds which are available both hulled and unhulled. In India, white sesame seeds are preferred for cooking purposes; sesame oil is used mainly in Southern India; and roasted sesame seeds are used for their nutty texture and aroma.

TAMARIND

Tamarind is sold in many forms in Asian shops. The pulp variety is the most convenient one to use for the recipes in this book.

TURMERIC

Ground turmeric is widely used in Indian cooking, both for its golden colour and its distinctive aroma. It is available in many supermarkets and Asian shops. It should be bought in small amounts and kept in a dark place.

URD BEANS / URID DAL

Urd beans are available, both whole and split, from Indian food shops.

Like the individual spices, these mixtures should all be stored in air-tight containers.

GARAM MASALA

This spice mixture is often used to finish Indian dishes. Everyone has their own recipe – here is one I find excellent.

1 tablespoon cardamom seeds
4 cm (1^1/$_2$ in) cinnamon stick
^{1}/$_4$ tablespoon black peppercorns
^{1}/$_4$ tablespoon cloves
^{1}/$_4$ tablespoon cumin seeds
^{1}/$_2$ tablespoon fennel seeds

Dry-roast all the spices in a heavy-based pan, then grind to a powder in a coffee grinder.

KASHMIRI MASALA

This is used in a lot of vegetarian dishes. I find the flavour subtle and not as overpowering as *garam masala.*

2 tablespoons fennel seeds
1 tablespoon cardamom seeds
6 bay leaves
2 teaspoons mace

Mix all the ingredients and grind to a powder in a coffee grinder. Make small quantities at a time.

PANCH PHORAN

Panch means 'five' in Bengali. This combination
of five whole spices is used in Bengal to flavour
vegetables and fish dishes.

1 tablespoon mustard seeds
1 tablespoon cumin seeds
1 tablespoon kalonji
1/4 tablespoon fenugreek seeds
1/2 tablespoon fennel seeds

Mix all the ingredients together.

PICKLING SPICES

1 tablespoon cumin seeds
1 tablespoon black cumin seeds
1 tablespoon kalonji
1/2 tablespoon mustard seeds

Mix all the ingredients together.

BASIC METHODS OF COOKING

Preparing food is a good way of expressing one's creativity. Colour, texture and flavour are important things to look for when creating any dish. The Indian housewife cooks not just to feed but also to delight.

It is best to cut up the vegetables and arrange your ingredients beforehand, as Indian cooking usually involves adding one ingredient after another in quick succession. The most important factor in all Indian cooking is temperature control. The basic cooking techniques are explained below.

BOILING

Some foods, like rice, potatoes and some vegetables, can simply be boiled. For plain boiled rice, the best variety to use is patna long-grain. Cook it, like pasta, in salted water with a teaspoon of oil and drain in a colander.

SIMMERING

Lentils, casserole dishes and curry dishes are cooked by simmering over a low heat. By simmering you can extract the optimum amount of flavour and incorporate the spices into the food.

STIR-FRYING

Most vegetables can be cooked in a little oil over a high heat. Slow-cooking vegetables are added first and faster-cooking vegetables are added later. Towards the end of the cooking time, a little liquid is added so that the vegetables cook properly and remain moist. This is probably the best way to cook vegetables.

SHALLOW-FRYING

Shallow frying is done in a frying pan with very little fat. In India, spiced vegetable cutlets and other such delicacies are shallow-fried.

DEEP-FRYING

Perhaps the most commonly deep-fried items are vegetable fritters, cottage cheese fritters, and breads like *pooris*. Deep-frying is ideally done in a *karai* (a heavy wok-like vessel), as it requires less oil and fries the food evenly. However, a deep-fat fryer or deep non-stick frying pan would do equally well.

TEMPERING

Tempering is very important in Indian cooking. It is a process whereby whole spices are dropped into hot oil or ghee. While sizzling and changing colour, the spices release their fragrance which is absorbed by the oil. Tempering is usually done before putting in the other ingredients. In other cases it is done after the cooking is complete and the aromatic oil is poured over the dish.

SOUPS AND STARTERS

In India, soups and starters are not served as separate courses as they are in the West. When entertaining, you may wish to serve a selection of these dishes – they are all delicious and very quick and easy to cook. Most of the soups can be made well in advance and re-heated before serving, whereas the fried items should be freshly cooked.

SPICED YOGHURT SOUP
DAHI SHORBA

This soup is wonderfully cool and refreshing in hot Delhi summers.

Process the chillies, onion, ginger and garlic until finely chopped. Heat the ghee in a saucepan and temper with the cumin, mustard seeds and curry leaves. When they begin to splutter, add the fresh spices and fry until brown. Add the turmeric and fry for a further 30 seconds. Whisk together the yoghurt and the cream until smooth and add to the pan. Season to taste with sugar and salt, and keep whisking slowly until the soup comes to the boil. Remove from the heat, garnish with the chopped fresh coriander, and serve. The sugar content should be varied according to the sourness of the yoghurt and personal taste.

INGREDIENTS

PREPARATION TIME
10 minutes
COOKING TIME
10 minutes

2 green chillies
1 large onion, peeled and
roughly chopped
1 cm (¹/₂ in) fresh ginger,
peeled
5 cloves garlic, peeled
2 tablespoons ghee
¹/₄ tablespoon cumin seeds
¹/₄ tablespoon mustard seeds
A few curry leaves
¹/₄ tablespoon ground
turmeric
300 ml (10 fl oz) plain
yoghurt
300 ml (10 fl oz) cream
¹/₄–¹/₂ tablespoon sugar
Salt
1 tablespoon chopped fresh
coriander

SPINACH SOUP
PALAK SAAR

A rich spinach soup which is a favourite of the Marathi Brahmins who live in the coastal regions of Western India.

Remove the stalks from the spinach and chop the leaves. Wash in cold water and drain in a colander. Blend the green chillies, ginger and garlic to a paste, adding a little water if necessary to blend. Heat the ghee in a saucepan and temper with the mustard seeds, whole red chillies and bay leaves. Add the chilli, ginger and garlic paste and fry for 1–2 minutes. Then add the spinach and fry for a further 2–3 minutes. Add the flour and mix. Add the coconut milk, 200 ml (10 fl oz) water and salt to taste. Bring to the boil, reduce the heat and simmer for 10 minutes until the soup has thickened. Serve hot.

INGREDIENTS

PREPARATION TIME
10 minutes
COOKING TIME
15–20 minutes

1 bunch of fresh spinach
3 green chillies
2.5 cm (1 in) fresh ginger, peeled
6 cloves garlic, peeled
2 tablespoons ghee
¹/₄ tablespoon mustard seeds
2 whole dried red chillies
2 bay leaves
2 tablespoons plain flour
300 ml (10 fl oz) coconut milk
Salt

GREEN SOUP
CALDO VERDE

Goa, on the west coast of India, was a Portuguese colony for hundreds of years. This Goan soup is an unusual blend of the two cuisines.

Heat the oil in a saucepan, temper with the bay leaves, then sauté the onion. Meanwhile, process the ginger and chillies for a few seconds. When the onions are soft, add the ginger, chillies and potatoes. Sauté for a few minutes and add the stock or water. Leave to simmer until the potatoes are nearly done. Add the spinach and tomato. Season to taste with salt and leave to simmer until all the vegetables are cooked. Serve hot.

INGREDIENTS

PREPARATION TIME
10 minutes
COOKING TIME
20 minutes

*1 tablespoon oil
3 bay leaves
1 large onion, peeled and chopped
1 cm (¹/₂ in) fresh ginger, peeled
2 green chillies
2 medium potatoes, peeled and cut into 1 cm (¹/₂ in) cubes
600 ml (1 pint) vegetable stock or water
¹/₂ bunch fresh spinach, washed and cut into strips
1 medium tomato, skinned and quartered
Salt*

Pumpkin Soup

KADHU SHORBA

The pumpkin is a very common vegetable in India and every region has different ways of cooking it. In Bengal they often have pumpkin fritters, whereas in the South it is usually cooked with coconut. This recipe is from the Gymkhana Club in Delhi. Although it takes longer to make than most of the other soups, it is very good for freezing and can be made a day in advance.

Heat the oil in a saucepan and cook the onion with the bay leaves for 3–4 minutes. Meanwhile process the ginger, garlic and chilli for a few seconds, then add to the pan and stir-fry for 1 minute. Now add the pumpkin and sauté for 2–3 minutes. Add the tomato, chopped coriander and stock, and simmer for 25–30 minutes. Leave to cool for a few minutes, then purée in a blender. Add a little more stock to thin if necessary. Re-heat before serving, adding the cream, and lemon juice and salt to taste.

INGREDIENTS

PREPARATION TIME
12 minutes
COOKING TIME
40 minutes

2 tablespoons oil
1 medium onion, peeled and chopped
2 bay leaves
1 cm ($^1/_2$ in) fresh ginger, peeled
2 cloves garlic, peeled
1 green chilli
450 g (1 lb) pumpkin, peeled and diced
1 medium tomato, skinned and chopped
1 tablespoon chopped fresh coriander
750 ml (1$^1/_4$ pints) vegetable stock
4 tablespoons single cream
Lemon juice
Salt

TOMATO AND COCONUT SOUP
TAMATAR AUR NARIAL SHORBA

A refreshing soup from the south coast of India.

Roughly chop the tomatoes and set aside. Heat the butter in a saucepan and drop in the bay leaves and chopped onion. Sauté until the onion is tender, add the flour and fry for 1–2 minutes. Add the chopped tomatoes and grated or desiccated coconut and fry for a further 2–3 minutes. Process the chillies and ginger for a few seconds and add to the pan. Pour in 500 ml (18 fl oz) water and season to taste with salt. Cook over a medium heat for 10–12 minutes, rub through a sieve and add the coconut milk. Boil for another few minutes to reduce further if the soup is too thin. Serve hot, garnished with the chopped fresh coriander.

INGREDIENTS

PREPARATION TIME
10 minutes
COOKING TIME
25–30 minutes

450 g (1 lb) tomatoes
2 tablespoons butter
3 bay leaves
1 large onion, peeled and chopped
2 tablespoons plain flour
100 g (4 oz) grated or desiccated coconut
2 green chillies
2.5 cm (1 in) fresh ginger, peeled
Salt
65 ml (2¹/₂ fl oz) coconut milk
1 tablespoon chopped fresh coriander

Pepper and
Tamarind Consomme
KALA MIRCH AUR IMLI RASAM

This very thin vegetarian consommé from the south coast is usually served on cold nights and also as an aid to digestion at the beginning or end of a meal.

Dissolve the tamarind in 65 ml (2½ fl oz) warm water. Put this water in a saucepan and add the tomato, whole red chillies, turmeric, peppercorns, cumin seeds, asafoetida and 600 ml (1 pint) water. Bring to the boil, then reduce the heat and leave to simmer for 10 minutes. Meanwhile, heat the ghee in a pan and temper with the mustard seeds and curry leaves. When the spices are about to change colour, add them to the consommé. Serve hot, garnished with the chopped fresh coriander.

INGREDIENTS

PREPARATION TIME
*3 minutes plus 10 minutes
soaking time for tamarind*
COOKING TIME
15 minutes

---

1 tablespoon tamarind pulp
*1 medium tomato, skinned
and quartered*
2 whole dried red chillies
*½ tablespoon ground
turmeric*
*1 tablespoon black
peppercorns, crushed*
*½ tablespoon cumin seeds,
crushed*
A pinch of asafoetida
1 tablespoon ghee
¼ tablespoon mustard seeds
6 curry leaves
*1 tablespoon chopped fresh
coriander*

PAKORAS

INGREDIENTS

PREPARATION TIME
10 minutes
COOKING TIME
6 minutes per batch of 3–4

*500 g (1¹/₄ lb) mixed
vegetables
Salt
1 tablespoon ground
turmeric
225 g (8 oz) chickpea flour
1 tablespoon chilli powder
¹/₂ tablespoon cumin seeds
1 tablespoon ground
coriander
¹/₄ tablespoon ajwain seeds
2 tablespoons white vinegar
Oil to deep-fry*

This is a snack one usually has in roadside cafés in Delhi. Any type of vegetable can be fried in batter, but the most popular ones are potatoes, cauliflower, aubergine, green peppers, green chillies and onions.

Cut the round vegetables (such as onions and aubergines) into thin slices; cut all the other vegetables into 2.5 cm (1 in) cubes. Rub with salt and ¹/₂ tablespoon ground turmeric, and set aside. Put the chickpea flour into a mixing bowl with the rest of the turmeric, the chilli powder, cumin seeds, ground coriander, ajwain seeds and vinegar, and mix. Add 85–120 ml (3–4 fl oz) water to make a smooth coating batter with seeds.

Heat the oil to a medium temperature in a *karai* or deep frying pan. Put a handful of mixed vegetables in the batter and mix well until coated all over. Put 3–4 vegetables at a time into the oil and fry until crisp and golden. Remove and drain on absorbent paper. Serve hot, with a spicy chutney such as Date and Tamarind (page 102) or Tomato and Chilli (page 105).

CHANNA DAL FRITTERS
CHANNA DAL BHAJIAS

This is a nice way to start a vegetarian meal. (If *channa dal* is unavailable you can substitute yellow split peas.) The *bhajias* should be served warm with a tangy Coconut Chutney (page 108).

━━━━━━━

Drain the *dal* well and pat dry with a kitchen towel. Process or put through the medium blade of a mincer with all the ingredients except the cumin seeds. (Do not add any water.) Beat the mixture, which should be fairly stiff, and add the cumin seeds. Form the dough into balls about half the size of golf balls and flatten them so that they look more like thickish discs. Heat the oil to a medium heat in a *karai* or deep frying pan, drop the *bhajias* in and cook until golden brown.

INGREDIENTS

PREPARATION TIME
12 minutes plus overnight soaking time for dal
COOKING TIME
15–20 minutes

250 g (9 oz) channa dal, washed and soaked overnight
$^1/_2$ tablespoon bicarbonate of soda
1 small onion, peeled and chopped
6 cloves garlic, peeled
1 green chilli
1 cm ($^1/_2$ in) fresh ginger, peeled
A few mint leaves
A few curry leaves
1 tablespoon coriander leaves
$^1/_2$ tablespoon ground turmeric
A pinch of salt
$^1/_2$ tablespoon cumin seeds
Oil to deep-fry

CRISPY SAGO DUMPLINGS

SABU BONDAS

PREPARATION TIME
6–8 minutes plus 30 minutes standing time for sago
COOKING TIME
6–8 minutes

175 g (6 oz) sago
100 g (4 oz) rice flour
175 g (6 oz) plain flour
6 green chillies
2.5 cm (1 in) fresh ginger, peeled
1 tablespoon chopped fresh coriander
$^{1}/_{4}$ tablespoon ajwain seeds
Salt to taste
Oil to deep-fry

A simple yet very unusual dish.

Mix the sago, rice flour and plain flour in a bowl. Add enough water to make a semi-hard dough and leave to rest for about 30 minutes.

Meanwhile process the chillies and ginger for a few seconds. Then, add the rest of the ingredients and form into balls about half the size of golf balls. Heat the oil in a *karai* or deep frying pan, and fry over a medium heat until nice and golden on the outside. Serve with any tangy dip or chutney (pages 94–108).

CRISPY FRIED
SEMOLINA PATTIES
RAVA VADAS

A delicious savoury dish from the west coast of India, semolina *vadas* can be served either as an entrée or a side dish.

———

Whisk the yoghurt and add the semolina. Set aside for 30 minutes. Process the onion, chillies and ginger for a few seconds.

Mix all the ingredients together to form a stiff dough. If the mixture is too dry, sprinkle with a little water and knead until thoroughly amalgamated. Form into balls about half the size of golf balls. Heat the oil to a medium temperature in a *karai* or deep frying pan. Flatten the balls into patties and fry over a medium heat until golden brown. Serve with Mint and Coriander Dip (page 97).

INGREDIENTS

PREPARATION TIME
10 minutes plus 30 minutes standing time
COOKING TIME
8 minutes per batch of 8

250 ml (8 fl oz) plain yoghurt
350 g (12 oz) fine semolina
1 large onion, peeled
4 green chillies
2.5 cm (1 in) fresh ginger, peeled
1 tablespoon chopped fresh coriander
1 tablespoon black peppercorns, crushed
2 tablespoons cashew nuts, broken
2 tablespoons grated or desiccated coconut
Salt to taste
Oil to deep-fry

CRISPY FRIED
BEETROOT PATTIES
BEET VADAS

INGREDIENTS

PREPARATION TIME
10 minutes
COOKING TIME
*10 minutes per batch of
8–10*

*2 green chillies, chopped
2.5 cm (1 in) fresh ginger,
peeled
A few fresh coriander
leaves
2 beetroot, peeled
100 g (4 oz) chickpea flour
2 tablespoons grated or
desiccated coconut
2 tablespoons cashew nuts,
broken
¹/₄ tablespoon ground
turmeric
Breadcrumbs to coat
Oil to deep-fry*

Beetroot's deep purple colour makes it look very appealing. In India this vegetable is used in many ways, the most common being to make *vadas* which can be served as an entrée, snack or side dish.

Process the chillies, ginger and coriander for a few seconds. Grate the beetroot, in a food processor, if desired. Put the fresh spices and beetroot in a bowl and mix in all the other ingredients to make a soft dough, adding water if required. Form into balls about half the size of golf balls and roll in breadcrumbs.

Heat the oil to a medium temperature in a *karai* or deep frying pan, and drop in as many *vadas* as you can fit in, usually 8–10. Fry until golden brown and crisp. Serve with a sweet and sour Apple Chutney (page 107).

SPINACH SOUP (*PALAK SAAR*) PAGE 23, AND SPICED YOGHURT SOUP (*DAHI SHORBA*) PAGE 22

SALADS

Salads form an important part of many Indian vegetarian meals. People often just have thinly sliced raw onions with their lunch, but they have rather more exotic salads with dinner. Leafy vegetables tend to be served as cooked greens rather than raw; soaked or sprouted beans are more usual salad ingredients. In the Punjab, salads are mostly tossed with lemon juice and one or two spices, whereas in South India, raw vegetables are usually flavoured with a little spiced oil.

PAKORAS (PAGE 28) WITH MINT CHUTNEY (*PUDINA CHUTNEY*) PAGE 101

CARROT AND YOGHURT SALAD
GAJJAR KOCHUMBARI

INGREDIENTS

PREPARATION TIME
10 minutes
COOKING TIME
2 minutes

100 g (4 oz) carrots,
peeled
150 ml (5 fl oz) plain
yoghurt
2 green chillies, chopped
1 tablespoon sugar
20 g (³/₄ oz) roasted
peanuts, ground
¹/₂ tablespoon oil
¹/₂ tablespoon mustard seeds
¹/₂ tablespoon cumin seeds
A few curry leaves
(optional)
1 tablespoon chopped fresh
coriander to garnish

A characteristic Maharashtrian way of eating yoghurt, usually served as a side dish.

Grate the carrots using a grater or food processor. Beat the yoghurt and stir in the carrots, chillies, sugar and ground peanuts. Set aside. Heat the oil in a pan and temper with the mustard seeds, cumin seeds, and curry leaves, if using. When the spices start spluttering, add them to the yoghurt mixture. Serve chilled, garnished with the chopped fresh coriander.

TANGY CARROT SALAD
GAJJAR KOSUMALLI

A simple and very refreshing carrot salad from South India.

Finely grate the carrots using a grater or food processor. Put in a mixing bowl and add salt and lime juice to taste. Heat the oil in a small pan and temper with the mustard seeds, curry leaves and asafoetida. Add the oil and spices to the salad. Serve at once.

INGREDIENTS

PREPARATION TIME
7 minutes
COOKING TIME
2 minutes

250 g (9 oz) carrots,
peeled
Salt
Juice of 1 lime
1 tablespoon oil
$^1/_4$ tablespoon mustard seeds
A few curry leaves
A pinch of asafoetida

MUNG BEAN, LETTUCE AND TOMATO SALAD
MOONG DAL KOSUMALLI

A healthy yet delicious way to eat whole mung beans. One can sprout the beans at home or buy them ready-sprouted from a health food shop.

INGREDIENTS

PREPARATION TIME
7 minutes
COOKING TIME
5 minutes

1 cos or iceberg lettuce
1 tablespoon oil
1/4 tablespoon mustard seeds
2 green chillies, chopped
2 tablespoons grated or desiccated coconut
150 g (5 oz) sprouted mung beans (page 14)
Juice of 1 lime
Salt
2 small tomatoes, quartered
1/2 tablespoon black peppercorns, crushed

Wash the lettuce, leave it to drain and cut into salad-size pieces. Arrange in a serving dish and keep in a cool place.

Heat the oil in a pan and temper with the mustard seeds, green chillies and 1 tablespoon coconut. Add the sprouted mung beans and warm slowly on a medium heat. Just heat through; do not cook. Add lime juice and salt to taste. Sprinkle the beans over the lettuce and throw in the tomatoes and crushed peppercorns. Serve at once, garnished with the remaining coconut.

Mung bean, potato and tomato salad

MOONG KI CHAT

A very popular mung bean salad usually eaten as a road-side snack in Delhi.

Process the onion, chilli and fresh coriander for a few seconds, then mix with the remaining ingredients. Season to taste with lemon juice and salt, and serve.

INGREDIENTS

PREPARATION TIME
6 minutes plus boiling time for potato

1 medium onion, peeled and roughly chopped
1 green chilli
1 tablespoon coriander leaves
250 g (9 oz) sprouted mung beans (page 14)
1 medium potato, peeled, boiled and diced
1 medium tomato, diced
1 tablespoon chat masala
Lemon juice
Salt

POTATO SALAD
WITH POMEGRANATE
ALOO CHAMAN KI CHAT

A very exotic cold salad from the Punjab, influenced by the cuisine of the Hindu Kush mountains where they grow the best pomegranates. Using a pressure cooker for the potatoes makes this a very quick and easy dish.

INGREDIENTS

PREPARATION TIME
*12 minutes plus boiling
time for potatoes*

*4 green chillies, chopped
2 tablespoons chopped fresh
coriander
150 ml (5 fl oz) soured
cream
350 g (12 oz) potatoes,
peeled, boiled and diced
Salt
Lemon juice (optional)
200 g (7 oz) pomegranate
seeds*

Put the chopped chillies and 1 tablespoon chopped coriander in a mixing bowl with the soured cream. Mix in the cooled potatoes, season to taste with salt, and add lemon juice if required. Put in a serving dish and sprinkle the pomegranate seeds over the top. Serve chilled, garnished with the remaining fresh coriander.

MAIN MEALS

The various elements of a complete and balanced Indian vegetarian meal are set down in the holy scriptures. No vegetarian meal is complete without milk or at least one milk product. Usually, three to four dishes are served. Rice or bread form the basic staple, accompanied by one *dal*, one green vegetable and one seasonal vegetable. A yoghurt side dish or dessert is a must. As a general rule a meal served with rice is accompanied with a couple of wet main dishes, and perhaps a couple of dry side dishes. If, however, the meal is to be served with breads the main dishes should be dry ones.

But this should only be regarded as a rough guide and you should really experiment with the recipes and follow your own instincts.

CABBAGE WITH COCONUT
COS ERISSERY

PREPARATION TIME
12 minutes
COOKING TIME
10 minutes

1 tablespoon chickpea flour
450 g (1 lb) white cabbage,
shredded
2 tablespoons oil
¹/₂ tablespoon mustard seeds
¹/₂ tablespoon whole black
peppercorns
A pinch of asafoetida
3 green chillies, slit
2.5 cm (1 in) fresh ginger,
chopped
A few curry leaves
¹/₂ tablespoon ground
turmeric
¹/₂ tablespoon sugar
2 tablespoons grated or
desiccated coconut
2 tablespoons cashew nuts,
crushed

This dish comes from Kerala, the cashew and pepper country of India.

Mix the chickpea flour with 65 ml (2¹/₂ fl oz) water and set aside. Blanch or steam the cabbage until soft. Remove from the heat and drain in a colander.

Heat the oil in a pan and temper with the mustard seeds, peppercorns and asafoetida. Now add the green chillies, ginger, curry leaves, steamed cabbage, turmeric, sugar and coconut, and stir-fry for 2–3 minutes. Gradually stir in the chickpea flour and water mixture and keep stirring until all the moisture has evaporated. Serve hot, garnished with the crushed cashew nuts.

SPICY GREEN TOMATOES
TAMATAR PITLA

A robust earthy dish from the western hinterland of India.

Process the chillies and ginger for a few seconds. Now mix the chickpea flour with 150 ml (5 fl oz) water and whisk until smooth. Heat the ghee or oil in a pan and temper with the bay leaves and dry spices. When they start changing colour, add the chillies, ginger and tomatoes and stir-fry for 2–3 minutes. Now add the chickpea flour mixture and keep stirring until it comes to the boil. Reduce the heat and simmer gently until the tomatoes are soft and the sauce has thickened. Garnish with the chopped fresh coriander and serve.

INGREDIENTS

PREPARATION TIME
8 minutes
COOKING TIME
15 minutes

*6 green chillies
2.5 cm (1 in) fresh ginger, peeled
1 tablespoon chickpea flour
2 tablespoons ghee or oil
3 bay leaves
$^1/_4$ tablespoon mustard seeds
$^1/_4$ tablespoon cumin seeds
$^1/_4$ tablespoon fenugreek seeds
$^1/_4$ tablespoon kalonji seeds
$^1/_2$ tablespoon ground turmeric
8 green tomatoes, quartered
1 tablespoon chopped fresh coriander*

SPINACH WITH PEAS & BEANS
PALAK SAAS

No meal is complete without a green leafy vegetable. This is a delicious spinach dish of the Marathi Brahmins who are very strict vegetarians.

This recipe works well with frozen spinach. If using fresh, remove the stalks and wash, then cut into fine strips. Cut the green beans into bite-size pieces. If using other large vegetables, cut into small cubes.

Heat the oil in a saucepan and temper with the mustard seeds. Add the onion and sauté until soft. Process the ginger and chillies for a few seconds. Then add them to the pan with the turmeric, peanuts and chickpea flour. Fry for 2–3 minutes, then add the vegetables and spinach. Keep stirring until all the spices and vegetables are amalgamated. Bring to the boil, then reduce the heat. Season to taste with salt and simmer gently, stirring occasionally, until the liquid has reduced and the dish is semi-dry.

INGREDIENTS

PREPARATION TIME
10 minutes using frozen spinach
COOKING TIME
15–20 minutes

250 g (9 oz) defrosted frozen spinach or 2 bunches fresh spinach
120 g (4¹/₂ oz) green beans
2 tablespoons oil
¹/₂ tablespoon mustard seeds
1 large onion, peeled and chopped
2.5 cm (1 in) fresh ginger, peeled
4 green chillies
¹/₂ tablespoon ground turmeric
50 g (2 oz) peanuts
1 tablespoon chickpea flour
120 g (4¹/₂ oz) green peas
Salt

Mushroom and Peas Korma
Khumbi aur Mattar Korma

Mushrooms and green peas are a tasty and colourful combination. This is a modern version of an old Mughal recipe.

Heat the oil in a pan and temper with the bay leaves. Add the onion and sauté until soft. Meanwhile process the ginger and garlic for a few seconds, then add to the pan, together with the turmeric and chilli powder. Fry for 1 minute, then add the soured cream and 120 ml (4 fl oz) water. Stir the mixture and bring to a fast boil, then reduce the heat and simmer. When the curry thickens, add the mushrooms and peas. Mix the ground almonds with enough water to make a paste and add to the curry. Cook until the mushrooms are tender and season to taste with salt. Add the *Kashmiri masala* and chopped fresh coriander, cook for a further minute and serve.

INGREDIENTS

PREPARATION TIME
7 minutes
COOKING TIME
15 minutes

2 tablespoons oil
3 bay leaves
1 large onion, peeled and chopped
2.5 cm (1 in) fresh ginger, peeled
2 cloves garlic, peeled
¹/₂ tablespoon ground turmeric
1 tablespoon chilli powder
120 ml (4 fl oz) soured cream
350 g (12 oz) button mushrooms, quartered
120 g (4¹/₂ oz) green peas
2 tablespoons ground almonds
Salt
1 tablespoon Kashmiri masala (page 17)
1 tablespoon chopped fresh coriander

FRIED OKRA
WITH TOMATOES
BHINDI DO PIAZA

Every Indian household has a different method of cooking okra. Here is one I like from Delhi.

Slice the stems off the okra and cut into bite-size pieces. Heat the oil in a deep frying pan and temper with the cumin seeds. Add the onion and fry until soft. Now add the okra, the remaining spices, and salt to taste. Lower the heat, cover and simmer, stirring occasionally. When the okra is tender, add the tomatoes, sprinkle with the *amchur* or lemon juice and toss. Serve hot.

INGREDIENTS

PREPARATION TIME
12 minutes
COOKING TIME
15 minutes

450 g (1 lb) okra
2 tablespoons oil
$^1/_2$ tablespoon cumin seeds
1 large onion, peeled and cut into 1 cm ($^1/_2$ in) cubes
2.5 cm (1 in) fresh ginger, peeled and grated
1 tablespoon ground coriander
$^1/_2$ tablespoon ground cumin
1 tablespoon chilli powder
Salt
2 small tomatoes, cut into wedges
1 tablespoon amchur or lemon juice

Maharaja's Aubergine
Ratatouille
Brinjal ka Salan

This delightful dish from the princely houses of Hyderabad is influenced by the coconut-based cuisine of the South.

———

Heat the oil in a deep frying pan and temper with the kalonji seeds. Add the onion and sauté until soft, then add the tomato and cook for 5–6 minutes over a medium heat. When the mixture begins to thicken, add the diced aubergines and stir-fry for 1–2 minutes. Cover and simmer until the aubergines are nearly cooked. Then slowly stir in the coconut milk. Let it simmer while you process the ginger, coriander leaves and seeds for a few seconds. Add the rest of the ingredients, except the nuts, and season to taste with salt. Serve hot, garnished with slivered almonds or pistachios, if preferred.

INGREDIENTS

PREPARATION TIME
10 minutes
COOKING TIME
15 minutes

2 tablespoons oil
¼ tablespoon kalonji seeds
1 large onion, peeled and chopped
1 large tomato, skinned and chopped
450 g (1 lb) aubergine, cut into 1 cm (½ in) cubes
85 ml (3 fl oz) coconut milk
2.5 cm (1 in) fresh ginger, peeled
1 tablespoon coriander leaves
½ tablespoon coriander seeds, crushed
½ tablespoon red chillies, crushed
Salt
A few slivered almonds or pistachio nuts (optional)

GREEN BEANS WITH GINGER AND CHILLIES

HARE BEANS KE SABZI

A dish from the Singaporean Tamils – a fusion of South Indian and South-East Asian cuisine.

Cut the beans into 2.5 cm (1 in) pieces and process the red chillies and ginger until finely chopped. Heat the oil in a pan with the crushed coriander seeds, red chillies and ginger. When the oil starts bubbling, add the beans, turmeric, and salt to taste. Stir-fry for 2–3 minutes, then add the coconut milk. Cook over a high heat until the dish is semi-dry. Serve hot, garnished with the chopped fresh coriander.

INGREDIENTS

PREPARATION TIME
7 minutes
COOKING TIME
12 minutes

*450 g (1 lb) green beans
5 dried red chillies,
de-seeded
2.5 cm (1 in) fresh ginger,
peeled
3 tablespoons oil
1 tablespoon coriander
seeds, crushed
$^1/_2$ tablespoon ground
turmeric
Salt
100 ml ($3^1/_2$ fl oz) coconut
milk
1 tablespoon chopped fresh
coriander*

CHUTNEY-COATED CAULIFLOWER
GOBI CHUTNEYWALI

This is an adaptation of a famous Parsi dish.

Blend all the chutney ingredients to a smooth paste. Break the cauliflower into medium-size florets, rub with salt and turmeric, and set aside.

In a pan with a tight-fitting lid, heat the oil and temper with the mustard seeds and bay leaves. Add the chutney and stir-fry for a further 2–3 minutes. Add the cauliflower and stir-fry for an additional 1–2 minutes. Check the seasoning, cover and reduce the heat. Simmer for 10–15 minutes until the cauliflower is nearly cooked. Uncover and let the moisture evaporate. Serve hot.

INGREDIENTS

PREPARATION TIME
12 minutes
COOKING TIME
15–20 minutes

FOR THE CHUTNEY
2 tablespoons fresh coriander leaves
2 tablespoons fresh mint leaves
2.5 cm (1 in) fresh ginger, peeled
6 cloves garlic
5 tablespoons grated or desiccated coconut
$^1/_2$ tablespoon cumin seeds
$^1/_2$ tablespoon coriander seeds
6 green chillies
$^1/_2$ tablespoon ground turmeric
$^1/_4$ tablespoon sugar

FOR THE CAULIFLOWER
450 g (1 lb) cauliflower
Salt
Ground turmeric
2 tablespoons oil
$^1/_2$ tablespoon mustard seeds
2 bay leaves

GREEN PEPPERS
GUJARATI-STYLE
SIMLA MIRCHI GUJARATI

PREPARATION TIME
7–10 minutes
COOKING TIME
10 minutes

450 g (1 lb) green peppers
3 tablespoons ghee or oil
¹/₂ tablespoon mustard seeds
A pinch of asafoetida
¹/₂ tablespoon sugar
¹/₂ tablespoon ground
turmeric
1 tablespoon chilli powder
1 tablespoon chickpea flour
or plain flour
¹/₂ tablespoon lemon or
lime juice
Salt

Green peppers are known as mountain peppers in India. They are usually cooked with other vegetables but this recipe from Gujarat (one of the vegetarian states of India) uses green peppers on their own.

De-seed the green peppers and cut into thick strips. Heat the ghee or oil in a deep frying pan and temper with the mustard seeds. Add the asafoetida and then the green peppers. Add the sugar and stir-fry for 2–3 minutes. Now add the turmeric and chilli powder and fry for another minute. Meanwhile, mix the flour with enough water to make a thin, smooth paste. Add this to the pan and stir-fry until the peppers are cooked. Stir in the lemon or lime juice and salt to taste.

COURGETTES COOKED IN PICKLING SPICES

COURGETTE ACHARI

This dish is adapted from a traditional recipe from Hyderabad.

Heat the ghee in a deep frying pan and temper with the pickling spices. Reduce the heat and add the ground turmeric, chilli powder and ground coriander. Sauté for 1 minute, then add the tomatoes. Increase the heat to medium and leave the tomatoes to cook. When the mixture has thickened, add the courgettes and salt to taste. Cook until the courgettes are soft. Process the ginger and chillies for a few seconds. Just before the end of the cooking time, add the ginger, chillies and *Kashmiri masala* and cook for a further minute. Serve hot, garnished with the chopped fresh coriander.

INGREDIENTS

PREPARATION TIME
10 minutes
COOKING TIME
12 minutes

2 tablespoons ghee
1 tablespoon pickling spices (page 18)
¹/₂ tablespoon ground turmeric
1 tablespoon chilli powder
¹/₂ tablespoon ground coriander
2 large tomatoes, skinned and chopped
450 g (1 lb) courgettes, diced
Salt
2.5 cm (1 in) fresh ginger, peeled
2 green chillies
¹/₂ tablespoon Kashmiri masala (page 17)
1 tablespoon chopped fresh coriander

CARROTS AND BEANS WITH COCONUT

GAJJAR AUR BEANS PODIAL

This is my version of a popular South Indian recipe.

INGREDIENTS

PREPARATION TIME
7 minutes
COOKING TIME
12 minutes

225 g (8 oz) carrots, cut into 4 cm (1¹/₂ in) pieces
225 g (8 oz) green beans, cut into 4 cm (1¹/₂ in) pieces
2 tablespoons oil
¹/₄ tablespoon mustard seeds
³/₄ tablespoon split urd beans
2 whole red chillies
4–6 curry leaves
3 tablespoons grated or desiccated coconut
2.5 cm (1 in) fresh ginger, peeled
2 green chillies
Lemon or lime juice
Salt

Cook the carrots and beans in boiling water until they are just soft yet still crunchy. Place under cold running water and leave in a colander to drain. Heat the oil in a *karai* or deep frying pan and temper with the mustard seeds. When they start spluttering, add the split urd beans, red chillies and curry leaves. Add half the coconut and fry for 1 minute. Then add the carrots and beans, and cook until the vegetables are heated through. Process the ginger and chillies for a few seconds, then add to the pan and cook for a further minute. Season to taste with lemon or lime juice and salt, garnish with the remaining coconut, and serve.

MUSHROOMS WITH COCONUT AND CORIANDER
KHUMBI DHANIYA

Fresh coriander and mushrooms make a very refreshing combination. This is an Indian adaptation of a French dish which is delightful served with pullao rice.

Whisk the yoghurt to a smooth consistency and mix with the coconut milk. Process the ginger and chillies for a few seconds. Then heat the ghee or oil in a deep frying pan and temper with the *panch phoran*, ginger and chillies. Add the mushrooms and stir-fry for 3–4 minutes. Add the turmeric, stir for a minute, then add the coconut and yoghurt. Stir gently until the mixture starts to boil. Then reduce the heat to medium and simmer until the sauce has thickened. Season to taste with salt, add the fenugreek leaves and chopped fresh coriander, cook for a further minute and serve.

INGREDIENTS

PREPARATION TIME
5 minutes
COOKING TIME
10 minutes

150 ml (5 fl oz) plain yoghurt
200 ml (7 fl oz) coconut milk
2.5 cm (1 in) fresh ginger, peeled
4 green chillies
2 tablespoons ghee or oil
1 tablespoon panch phoran (page 18)
450 g (1 lb) whole button mushrooms
¼ tablespoon ground turmeric
Salt
½ tablespoon dried fenugreek leaves
2 tablespoons chopped fresh coriander

SPICY STIR-FRIED PEAS
MATTAR BANJARA

INGREDIENTS

PREPARATION TIME
5 minutes
COOKING TIME
15 minutes

3 tablespoons ghee
¹/₂ tablespoon cumin seeds
2 whole dried red chillies
2 bay leaves
A pinch of asafoetida
2 medium onions, peeled
and chopped
1 tablespoon chilli powder
1 kg (2 lb) fresh or frozen
peas
Salt
1 tablespoon chopped fresh
ginger
1 tablespoon garam masala
(page 17)

Like green peppers, peas are normally cooked in combination with other vegetables in India. This is one of the very few recipes using them on their own.

Heat the ghee in a deep frying pan and temper with the cumin seeds, whole red chillies, bay leaves and asafoetida. When the spices are about to change colour, add the chopped onions and stir-fry until soft. Add the chilli powder and green peas. Now stir-fry for 1–2 minutes, sprinkle with a little water and cover. Cook for 3–4 minutes, then uncover. Reduce the heat and simmer until the peas are cooked. Just before the end of the cooking time, season to taste with salt, add the ginger and *garam masala*, cook for a further minute and serve.

SPICY PUNJABI TURNIPS
SHALGAM KA SALAN

An earthy winter vegetable dish from the Punjab, best served with hot Indian bread (pages 82–93).

Cut the turnips into quarters or eighths depending on their size. Sprinkle with a little salt and set aside for 10 minutes. Wash under cold running water and leave in a colander to drain.

Heat the ghee in a deep frying pan with a tight-fitting lid and temper with the *panch phoran* and bay leaves. Add the onions and stir-fry until soft. Add the chilli powder and fry for $1/2$ minute, then add the tomatoes and stir-fry for a further 4–5 minutes. Now add the turnips and sauté for 1–2 minutes. Reduce the heat, cover and simmer until tender.

When nearly done, uncover and add the crushed red chillies, coriander seeds, ginger and *Kashmiri masala*. Cook uncovered for 1–2 minutes. Serve hot.

INGREDIENTS

PREPARATION TIME
10 minutes plus 10 minutes standing time for turnips
COOKING TIME
15 minutes

450 g (1 lb) turnips, peeled
Salt
3 tablespoons ghee
2 tablespoons panch phoran (page 18)
3 bay leaves
2 large onions, peeled and chopped
$1^1/_2$ tablespoons chilli powder
3 medium tomatoes, skinned and chopped
2 red chillies, crushed
$1^1/_2$ tablespoons coriander seeds, crushed
1 tablespoon chopped fresh ginger
1 tablespoon Kashmiri masala (page 17)

BEANS AND LENTILS

Beans and lentils are the most common foods in India; there are about 50 types of lentil. Husked and split lentils are called *dal*, and this is also the name of the broth made from split lentils. *Dal*, in some form, is always present in an Indian vegetarian meal, as it is the richest source of protein in our diet.

Dals are at their best when soaked before cooking and cooked over a low heat for a long time. But it is not always possible to plan a meal so far in advance and there are some 'quick and easy' alternatives. The most obvious one is to use ready-cooked tinned pulses when available. However a pressure cooker can enable you to use dried pulses relatively quickly. Pressure cooking split lentils reduces their cooking time dramatically, with good results. But before cooking whole dried beans and chickpeas it is still essential to soak them overnight. When boiling pulses you should skim off the froth which forms on top from time to time. Leftover pulses can be puréed in a blender, then thinned or thickened with stock or water as required, to make a delightful and nutritious soup.

SPICY LENTILS
WITH VEGETABLES
TARKARI DAL

Each region in India has its own version of this vegetable *dal*. Many cook the *dal* and vegetables together and then purée the mixture, using it as a base for other curries. I personally like this Bengali variation in which the vegetables remain crunchy. Mixed vegetables can vary according to your preference but hard vegetables are most suited.

Put the *dal* in a heavy-based saucepan with 750 ml (1¹/₄ pints) water, the turmeric and salt to taste. Bring to the boil, then reduce the heat and simmer. Cover and cook for 10–12 minutes.

Meanwhile, heat the ghee in a frying pan and sauté the vegetables until they begin to soften. Add to the *dal* and simmer until the vegetables are tender. Process the ginger and chillies for a few seconds, then add to the pan together with the *Kashmiri masala*. Simmer for 1–2 minutes and serve garnished with the chopped fresh coriander.

INGREDIENTS

PREPARATION TIME
10 minutes
COOKING TIME
25–30 minutes

250 g (9 oz) split red lentils, washed and drained
¹/₂ tablespoon ground turmeric
Salt
3 tablespoons ghee
200 g (7 oz) mixed fresh vegetables (diced carrots, potatoes, green beans, peas or cauliflower florets)
2.5 cm (1 in) fresh ginger, peeled
2 green chillies
¹/₂ tablespoon Kashmiri masala (page 17)
1 tablespoon chopped fresh coriander

Urd bean dal

URID DAL

A country-style semi-dry *dal* which goes well with any Indian bread (pages 82–93).

PREPARATION TIME
5 minutes
COOKING TIME
15–20 minutes

250 g (9 oz) split urd beans, washed and drained
A pinch of salt
4 green chillies
2.5 cm (1 in) fresh ginger, peeled
3 tablespoons ghee
¹/₂ tablespoon cumin seeds
¹/₂ tablespoon fennel seeds
A pinch of asafoetida
1 tablespoon chopped fresh coriander

Put the *dal* in a saucepan with enough water to reach 5 cm (2 in) above it. Add the salt, cover and cook over a low heat for 10–15 minutes.

Meanwhile process the chillies and ginger for a few seconds. When the *dal* is nearly cooked, heat the ghee in a frying pan and temper with the cumin seeds, fennel seeds, asafoetida, chillies and ginger. Add this mixture to the *dal*, cover and simmer over a low heat for 5 minutes. Serve hot, garnished with the chopped fresh coriander.

Mung bean dal

SINDHI MOONG DAL

A lthough the mung beans have to be soaked overnight, the recipe itself is very simple.

Drain the *dal*, put it in a saucepan with 450 ml (15 fl oz) water, cover with a tight-fitting lid and cook over a medium heat for 15–20 minutes.

Meanwhile heat the ghee in a frying pan and temper with the garlic, cardamom, cloves and cinnamon. Add the onion, sauté until soft, then add the chilli powder and fry for 1 minute. Add this mixture to the *dal* and stir in the tamarind pulp. Cook for a further 10 minutes and season to taste with salt. If the *dal* is too thin, remove the lid and simmer until reduced. Serve garnished with the chopped fresh coriander.

INGREDIENTS

PREPARATION TIME
5 minutes plus overnight soaking time for mung beans
COOKING TIME
30–35 minutes

---

225 g (8 oz) split green mung beans, washed and soaked overnight
2 tablespoons ghee
5 cloves garlic, peeled
4 green cardamom pods
2 cloves
2.5 cm (1 in) cinnamon stick
1 large onion, peeled and chopped
1 tablespoon chilli powder
1 tablespoon tamarind pulp
Salt
1 tablespoon chopped fresh coriander

TANGY CHICKPEAS
CHANNA MASALA

PREPARATION TIME
7 minutes
COOKING TIME
15 minutes

*1 × 425 g (15 oz) tin
chickpeas
3 tablespoons ghee
2 bay leaves
1 tablespoon chilli powder
1 tablespoon ground
coriander
1 tablespoon ground cumin
1 teaspoon ground turmeric
2.5 cm (1 in) fresh ginger,
peeled
2 green chillies
1 tablespoon amchur or
lemon juice
Salt
2 tablespoons chopped fresh
coriander*

Chickpeas are a very popular festive dish in India. They are cooked in many different ways, both 'wet' and 'dry', and are usually eaten with rice or bread, depending on the occasion. In this recipe I have used the pre-cooked tinned variety. If using dried, you will need about 225 g (8 oz) chickpeas, soaked overnight and cooked for about 45 minutes until tender.

Wash the chickpeas under cold running water and leave to drain in a colander. Heat the ghee in a heavy-based saucepan and add the bay leaves, chilli powder, ground coriander, cumin and turmeric. Stir over a low heat until the mixture is dark brown, taking care that it does not burn. Add the chickpeas and stir-fry for a minute. Add 150 ml (5 fl oz) water and when it comes to the boil reduce the heat and simmer gently for about 5 minutes until thickened.

Process the ginger and chillies for a few seconds, then add to the pan with the amchur or lemon juice. Season to taste with salt, remove the bay leaves and serve garnished with the chopped fresh coriander.

WHOLE URD BEANS

SABUT URID

Whole beans are full of protein and goodness and therefore form a very important part of a balanced vegetarian meal. Though they are at their best when cooked slowly, a pressure cooker can make this dish much quicker and easier.

———

Rinse the beans 2–3 times in cold water. Put in a heavy-based saucepan with 1 tablespoon ginger, 2 cloves crushed garlic and the green chillies. Cover and bring to the boil, then reduce the heat and simmer for $1^{1}/_{2}$–2 hours until the beans are cooked. If using a pressure cooker, cook for 20–25 minutes, remove from heat, and let the pressure drop by itself.

Heat the ghee in a frying pan and temper with the cumin seeds, the remaining ginger and garlic and the red chillies. Add this to the beans, simmer for 15 minutes, sprinkle over the *Kashmiri masala*, and serve garnished with the chopped fresh coriander.

INGREDIENTS

PREPARATION TIME
10–15 minutes plus overnight soaking time for beans
COOKING TIME
25–30 minutes using a pressure cooker

250 g (9 oz) whole urd beans, washed and soaked overnight
2 tablespoons chopped fresh ginger
Salt
4 cloves garlic, peeled and crushed
3 green chillies, chopped
3 tablespoons ghee
$^{1}/_{2}$ tablespoon cumin seeds
4 dried red chillies, broken into 2 halves
$^{1}/_{2}$ tablespoon Kashmiri masala (page 17)
2 tablespoons chopped fresh coriander

POTATO DISHES

Potatoes are the single favourite food of most vegetarians. Actually, in any cuisine potatoes are cooked in more varied ways than any other vegetable, or meat for that matter. In India, every region has hundreds of recipes for potatoes. I have selected a few varied recipes for this chapter which are both unusual and easy to make.

MOGHULAI POTATOES

ALOO KA SALAN

This deliciously rich dish comes from the princely state of Hyderabad.

Heat the oil in a *karai* or deep frying pan and temper with the red chillies, mustard seeds, curry leaves and fenugreek seeds. When the spices start to change colour, add the diced parboiled potatoes and sauté for 3–4 minutes. Stir in the cream, bring to a fast boil, then reduce the heat and simmer until the cream is thick and the potatoes are tender, adding a little water if necessary. Process the ginger, green chillies and fresh coriander for a few seconds, then add to the pan and cook for a further minute. Season with salt to taste and serve.

INGREDIENTS

PREPARATION TIME
10 minutes
COOKING TIME
12 minutes

2 tablespoons oil
4 dried red chillies, broken into 2 halves
1/2 tablespoon mustard seeds
A few curry leaves
1/4 tablespoon fenugreek seeds
450 g (1 lb) potatoes, peeled, parboiled and cut into 1 cm (1/2 in) cubes
250 ml (8 fl oz) single cream
2.5 cm (1 in) fresh ginger, peeled
4 green chillies
2 tablespoons fresh coriander leaves
Salt

FRIED POTATOES
WITH MUSTARD
ALOO VADAKKAL

A favourite South Indian recipe which works particularly well in a non-stick pan, preferably a *karai* or wok.

INGREDIENTS

PREPARATION TIME
10 minutes
COOKING TIME
15 minutes

*450 g (1 lb) potatoes,
peeled and cut into 5 mm
(¹/₄ in) cubes
3 tablespoons oil
¹/₂ tablespoon black mustard
seeds
1 tablespoon split urd beans
A few curry leaves
¹/₄ tablespoon ground
turmeric
¹/₂ tablespoon chilli powder
A pinch of asafoetida
Lemon juice
Salt*

Wash the potatoes and leave to drain in a colander. Heat the oil in a non-stick pan and temper with the mustard seeds, urd beans and curry leaves. Add the potatoes and stir-fry for 2–3 minutes. Now add the turmeric, chilli powder and asafoetida and fry for a further 1–2 minutes. Sprinkle with about 2 tablespoons of water and continue to cook, stirring occasionally, until the potatoes are tender, adding a little more water if necessary. Leave on a low heat until the potatoes are crisp on the outside. Remove from the heat, and toss with lemon and salt to taste. Serve hot.

BENGALI-STYLE POTATOES
ALOO GOL MORICH

This very popular potato dish is usually eaten for brunch with *parathas* (page 92) or *rotis*. Many people leave out the peas but I think they look good with the potatoes.

Wash the potatoes and drain well in a colander. Heat the ghee in a heavy-based frying pan, *karai* or wok and temper with the *panch phoran*. When the spices change colour, add the potatoes and sauté for 3–4 minutes. Add salt to taste and fry for a further minute. Add 65 ml (2¹/₂ fl oz) water, cover and simmer until the potatoes are about three-quarters cooked. Add the peas and crushed peppercorns and stir lightly. Uncover and cook until the potatoes are tender. Serve hot, garnished with the chopped fresh coriander.

INGREDIENTS

PREPARATION TIME
8 minutes
COOKING TIME
15 minutes

---

450 g (1 lb) potatoes, peeled and cut into 2 cm (³/₄ in) cubes
2 tablespoons ghee
¹/₂ tablespoon panch phoran(page 18)
Salt
100 g (4 oz) fresh or frozen peas
1 tablespoon black peppercorns, crushed
1 tablespoon chopped fresh coriander

NEW POTATOES IN YOGHURT
ALOO DAHIWALA

PREPARATION TIME
10 minutes
COOKING TIME
*12 minutes plus boiling
time for potatoes*

*400 g (14 oz) new
potatoes
2 tablespoons oil or ghee
¹/₂ tablespoon cumin seeds
¹/₄ tablespoon kalonji seeds
¹/₂ tablespoon coriander
seeds, crushed
¹/₂ tablespoon ground
turmeric
200 ml (7 fl oz) plain
yoghurt, beaten
50 ml (2 fl oz) single
cream
2 green chillies
1 cm (¹/₂ in) fresh ginger,
peeled
2 tablespoons fresh
coriander leaves
Salt*

This is a tasty and unusual potato and yoghurt dish. The new potatoes can be eaten with or without their skins. If you want to peel them, do so after cooking and cooling.

Wash the new potatoes, then boil them in salted water until just cooked. Put them in a colander to drain and cool. (Do not rinse under cold water.)

Heat the oil or ghee in a *karai* or deep frying pan, and drop in the cumin seeds, kalonji seeds and coriander seeds. When the oil splutters, add the whole boiled potatoes and sauté for 2–3 minutes. Add the ground turmeric and sauté for a further 1–2 minutes. Now add the beaten yoghurt and cream and keep stirring slowly until the mixture comes to the boil. Simmer over a low heat for 2–3 minutes until the sauce thickens.

Process the chillies, ginger and fresh coriander for a few seconds, add to the pan and cook for a further minute. Season to taste with salt and serve.

OPPOSITE: CARROTS AND BEANS WITH COCONUT (*GAJJAR AUR BEANS PODIAL*) PAGE 52, POTATO SALAD WITH POMEGRANATE (*ALOO CHAMAN KI CHAT*) PAGE 40, AND MAHARAJA'S AUBERGINE RATATOUILLE (*BRINJAL KA SALAN*) PAGE 47
OVERLEAF: CARROT AND YOGHURT SALAD (*GAJJAR KOCHUMBARI*) PAGE 36, SPICY STIR-FRIED PEAS (*MATTAR BANJARA*) PAGE 54, AND MARATHI TOMATO RICE (*TAMATAR BHAT*) PAGE 86

POTATOES WITH COCONUT AND CASHEWS

ALOO PODIMAS

A dish from the coconut groves of Kerala in southern India.

Boil the potatoes in their jackets in salted water until they are almost cooked, then put them in a colander to drain and cool. (Do not rinse under cold water.) When cool, peel and cut them into 1 cm (¹/₂ in) cubes. Heat the oil in a deep frying pan and temper with urid dal, mustard seeds and curry leaves. Add the cashews and potatoes and stir-fry for 2–3 minutes. Process the ginger and chillies for a few seconds, then add to the pan, together with the coconut. Cook over a low heat and season with salt and lemon juice to taste. Serve hot.

INGREDIENTS

PREPARATION TIME
10 minutes
COOKING TIME
*10 minutes plus parboiling
time for potatoes*

400 g (14 oz) potatoes
3 tablespoons oil
¹/₂ tablespoon urid dal
¹/₂ tablespoon mustard seeds
A few curry leaves
*3 tablespoons cashew nuts,
halved*
*4 cm (1¹/₂ in) fresh ginger,
peeled*
2 green chillies
*3 tablespoons grated or
desiccated coconut*
Lemon juice
Salt

OPPOSITE: POTATOES WITH SPINACH (*ALOO PALAK*) PAGE 73, WITH
TOMATO AND CHILLI CHUTNEY (*TAMATAR AUR MIRCHI*) PAGE 105
PRECEDING PAGE: CHUTNEY-COATED CAULIFLOWER (*GOBI
CHUTNEYWALI*) (PAGE 49), CORN KERNELS WITH MIXED PEPPERS
(*BHUTTE KE DANE AUR SIMLA MIRCH*) PAGE 80, AND PLAIN BOILED RICE
(*SADHE CHAWAL*) PAGE 83

GOLDEN POTATOES
WITH ALMONDS
ALOO BADAMI

PREPARATION TIME
7 minutes
COOKING TIME
*12 minutes plus boiling
time for potatoes*

*350 g (12 oz) potatoes
2.5 cm (1 in) fresh ginger,
peeled
4 green chillies
3 tablespoons oil or ghee
$^1/_2$ tablespoon cumin seeds
$^1/_2$ tablespoon coriander
seeds, crushed
3 tablespoons slivered
almonds
Salt
$^1/_2$ tablespoon garam masala
(page 17)
1 tablespoon chopped fresh
coriander*

Potatoes and almonds make a nice combination, though you can use any type of nut for this dish, as long as it is skinned.

Boil the potatoes in their jackets in salted water until just cooked, then put them in a colander to drain and cool. (Do not rinse under cold water.) When cool, peel and cut them into 2 cm ($^3/_4$ in) cubes.

Process the ginger and chillies for a few seconds. Heat the oil or ghee in a deep frying pan and temper with the cumin seeds. When they are about to change colour, add the ginger, chillies, coriander seeds and slivered almonds. Stir-fry for 1 minute, then add the potatoes. Season to taste with salt and fry until the potatoes are crisp on the outside and slightly golden in colour.

Add the *garam masala*, cook for a further minute, and serve garnished with the chopped fresh coriander.

POTATOES WITH SPINACH
ALOO PALAK

A favourite winter dish from the Punjabi plains.

If using fresh spinach, remove the stalks and cut the leaves into fine strips. Wash under cold running water and leave in a colander to drain.

Heat the ghee in a deep frying pan and temper with the *panch phoran* and garlic. Add the onion and fry until soft. Add the turmeric and ground coriander and stir-fry for 1 minute, then add the tomatoes and cook for 2–3 minutes. Now add the potato and stir-fry for 2–3 minutes. Add the spinach and salt, reduce the heat and cook until the potatoes are soft. If the mixture becomes too dry, sprinkle a little water over the top.

Process the chillies and ginger for a few seconds, add to the pan and cook for a further minute. Serve hot.

INGREDIENTS

PREPARATION TIME
10 minutes using frozen spinach
COOKING TIME
15 minutes

*2 bunches fresh or 450 g
(1 lb) frozen spinach
2 tablespoons ghee
1 tablespoon panch phoran
(page 18)
4 cloves garlic, peeled and
crushed
1 large onion, peeled and
chopped
1/2 tablespoon ground
turmeric
1 tablespoon ground
coriander
3 medium tomatoes,
skinned and chopped
1 large potato, peeled and
cut into 1 cm (1/2 in) cubes
A pinch of salt
4 green chillies
2.5 cm (1 in) fresh ginger,
peeled*

ANGLO-INDIAN DISHES

Anglo-Indian cuisine is a fusion of Indian and English cuisine which originated in colonial times. When the *sahibs*, as the English were called, yearned for homely fare their cooks or *bawarchis* used to whip up something familiar with an Indian spice or two added for extra flavour. Though the cuisine was mostly meat-orientated, a number of vegetarian dishes also came to prominence. In this chapter I have included some of the most popular dishes from the old British Indian Army mess. Many of them are still very popular in India today.

CRISPY VEGETABLE ROLLS

Fried foods were very popular in the Army canteens, and rolls were a favourite snack because they were easy to eat. If you prefer, these rolls can be made with meat or fish fillings instead of vegetables. Spring roll skins are available at Chinese and Asian food shops, and you can save time by using pre-cut fresh vegetables sold in packets by supermarkets.

▬▬▬

Heat the oil in a deep frying pan and temper with the cumin seeds. Add the onion and sauté until soft. Add the vegetables and stir-fry until tender, then add the cream. Process the ginger and chillies for a few seconds, then add to the pan, together with the chilli powder and black pepper. Put the cornflour in a bowl and stir in enough water to make a liquid paste. Slowly stir the cornflour paste into the mixture, cook for 1 minute and leave to cool, then chill.

Lay out the spring roll skins in a diamond shape. Spoon two dollops of the chilled mixture on to one corner of each skin, fold in the other two corners and roll up. Brush with beaten egg to seal and deep-fry over a moderate heat until golden brown. Serve hot, garnished with the chopped fresh coriander.

INGREDIENTS

PREPARATION TIME
7 minutes using pre-cut vegetables plus cooling time
COOKING TIME
15 minutes

2 tablespoons oil
1/4 tablespoon cumin seeds
1 large onion, peeled and chopped
350 g (12 oz) mixed fresh vegetables (julienned carrots, beans, cauliflower florets, bean sprouts)
150 ml (5 fl oz) double cream
2.5 cm (1 in) fresh ginger, peeled
4 green chillies
1 tablespoon chilli powder
1/2 tablespoon black peppercorns, crushed
2 tablespoons cornflour
8 spring roll skins
1 egg, beaten
Oil to deep-fry
1 tablespoon chopped fresh coriander

75

FRIED SAVOURY PASTRIES

GAZA

This fried shortcrust pastry from South India keeps well and is usually served as a snack with tea or coffee.

INGREDIENTS

PREPARATION TIME
15 minutes plus 30 minutes resting time
COOKING TIME
5–7 minutes per batch of 10

450 g (1 lb) plain flour
A pinch of salt
2 tablespoons black cumin seeds
2 tablespoons ajwain seeds
3 tablespoons ghee
Oil to deep-fry

Sift the flour into a bowl with the salt and stir in the cumin and ajwain seeds. Heat the ghee in a small pan and rub into the flour until you get a texture resembling breadcrumbs. Now add 25–50 ml (1–2 fl oz) water to make a stiff rolling dough. Knead the dough until it leaves the sides of the bowl, cover with a wet cloth and leave to rest for about 30 minutes.

Form the dough into small balls and roll out thinly on a floured worktop or board. On each circle, make two shallow cuts 1 cm ($^1/_2$ in) apart and then again at right angles to form a diamond shape. Deep-fry over a moderate heat until the pastries are crisp and golden. Remove and drain on absorbent paper. When cool, store in an air-tight container.

GRILLED
MUSHROOMS

This recipe comes from a famous club in Calcutta where formal dress codes still apply. Patrons and guests are only admitted if attired in Western clothes.

Remove the mushroom stalks, set the caps aside, and chop the stalks. Heat the butter in a frying pan and sauté the onion until soft. Add the mushroom stalks and stir-fry for 1–2 minutes. Process the chillies and ginger for a few seconds, then add to the pan with the potatoes. Season to taste with lemon juice and salt, and add 1 tablespoon chopped fresh coriander.

Place the mushroom caps upside down on a greased baking tray and fill with the mixture. Put under the grill on a medium heat until the mushrooms are warmed through. Serve garnished with the remaining fresh coriander.

INGREDIENTS

PREPARATION TIME
*8 minutes plus boiling time
for potatoes*
COOKING TIME
15 minutes

16 large mushrooms
2 tablespoons butter
*1 medium onion, peeled
and chopped*
4 green chillies
*2.5 cm (1 in) fresh ginger,
peeled*
*2 medium potatoes, peeled,
boiled and cut into 1 cm
($^1/_2$ in) cubes*
Lemon juice
Salt
*2 tablespoons chopped fresh
coriander*

CHEESE CHILLI TOASTS

INGREDIENTS

PREPARATION TIME
6 minutes using ready-grated cheese
COOKING TIME
6 minutes

2 green chillies
2 tablespoons fresh coriander leaves
2.5 cm (1 in) fresh ginger, peeled
200 g (7 oz) freshly grated or ready-grated Cheddar cheese
1 egg
4 slices of white or brown bread, toasted
A few cocktail onions

A nother favourite of the Army *sahibs*, who used to have these canapés with their *chota pegs* (whisky and sodas).

Process the chillies, fresh coriander and ginger for a few seconds. Then put them in a bowl with the cheese and egg and mix to form a smooth paste. Divide equally between the four slices of toast, dipping a palette knife in water and smoothing the cheese topping. Place under the grill on a medium heat until the toast is heated through and golden on top. Remove the toast, cut into small bite-size pieces and serve garnished with a few cocktail onions.

CAULIFLOWER GRATIN

This Indian adaptation of baked cauliflower goes very well with a roasted or fried main dish. One can also use mixed vegetables in place of cauliflower.

Heat the oil or ghee in a heavy-based saucepan and temper with the bay leaves. Add the cauliflower and sauté for 2–3 minutes. Stir in the flour and sauté for a further 1–2 minutes. Add the milk and simmer, covered, until the cauliflower is about two-thirds cooked. Process the ginger and chillies for a few seconds, and add to the pan, together with the cashew nuts and black pepper. Mix gently and simmer until the cauliflower is just cooked.

Arrange the cauliflower in a flameproof serving dish, sprinkle the cheese on top and place under a hot grill until golden and bubbling. Serve hot, garnished with the chopped fresh coriander.

INGREDIENTS

PREPARATION TIME
10 minutes
COOKING TIME
20–25 minutes

2 tablespoons oil or ghee
2 bay leaves
450 g (1 lb) cauliflower,
broken into small florets
2 tablespoons plain flour
100 ml (3^1/$_2$ fl oz) milk
2.5 cm (1 in) fresh ginger,
peeled
3 green chillies
2 tablespoons cashew nuts,
crushed
^{1}/$_2$ tablespoon black
peppercorns, crushed
2 tablespoons freshly grated
Cheddar cheese
1 tablespoon chopped fresh
coriander

CORN KERNELS
WITH MIXED PEPPERS
BHUTTE KE DANE AUR SIMLA MIRCH

INGREDIENTS

PREPARATION TIME
10 minutes
COOKING TIME
12 minutes

2 tablespoons grated or desiccated coconut
4 green chillies
2.5 cm (1 in) fresh ginger, peeled
4 cloves garlic, peeled
2 tablespoons ghee or oil
¹/₂ tablespoon mustard seeds
1 medium red pepper, cut into 1 cm (¹/₂ in) squares
1 medium green pepper, cut into 1 cm (¹/₂ in) squares
400 g (14 oz) tinned or defrosted frozen sweetcorn
Salt

You can use either tinned or frozen sweetcorn for this dish but I prefer frozen.

Blend the coconut, chillies, ginger and garlic to a coarse paste, adding a little water if necessary. Heat the ghee or oil in a deep frying pan and temper with the mustard seeds. Add the spice paste and fry for 3–4 minutes. Now add the peppers and sweetcorn. Season to taste with salt, and stir-fry for a further 2–3 minutes. Reduce the heat and simmer until the peppers are just tender but still crunchy. Serve hot.

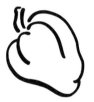

CRISPY FRIED POTATO, SAGO AND CHEESE PATTIES

SAGO ALOO VADAS

Another popular British Indian Army Club snack, and a good way of using up leftover mashed potato.

Put the sago in a bowl with enough water to cover it and leave to stand for 30 minutes.

Process the coriander, chillies and ginger for a few seconds, then put in a bowl with the cheese, potato, cornflour, roasted, broken peanuts and sago. Mix well and chill.

Form into balls about the size of a golfball, roll in breadcrumbs and place on greaseproof paper. Deep-fry the patties over a medium heat until they are golden brown. (Do not fry over a high heat as they will colour on the outside without cooking through.)

INGREDIENTS

PREPARATION TIME
7 minutes using ready-grated cheese, plus 30 minutes standing time
COOKING TIME
7 minutes per batch of 8

50 g (2 oz) sago
2 tablespoons fresh coriander leaves
3 green chillies
2.5 cm (1 in) fresh ginger, peeled
200 g (7 oz) freshly grated or ready-grated Cheddar cheese
250 g (9 oz) mashed potato
25 g (1 oz) cornflour
65 g (2¹/₂ oz) roasted peanuts, broken
Breadcrumbs to coat
Oil to deep-fry

RICE AND BREADS

R ice and breads are the perfect base for any Indian meal. Breads are generally formed into cones and used to scoop up the curry, and rice can be made in many interesting ways to complement different vegetable dishes. I have also included a recipe for rice noodles, which must be the fastest-cooking rice derivation available.

A word of advice about cooking rice: it is better to err on the side of too little water rather than too much. If the rice needs more water, sprinkle some on top, cover with a tight-fitting lid and leave in the oven at gas mark 3, 160°C (325°F), or on top of the cooker on a low heat. It will cook in the steam. Rice can be made well in advance and re-heated before serving.

Patna long-grain rice is the most commonly used variety and needs to be washed several times before cooking in order to get rid of the starch. If you use Basmati rice, a very fragrant variety, you will also need to soak it for at least 20 minutes before cooking. For other types of rice, follow the instructions on the packet. If brown rice is substituted for plain rice, cooking time and water should be adjusted.

PLAIN BOILED RICE
SADHE CHAWAL

This is the most basic method of cooking rice. Adding a bay leaf to the rice while cooking gives it a nice fragrance.

Put 900 ml (1¹/₂ pints) water in a saucepan over a high heat. When the water comes to the boil, add the bay leaves, salt and oil. Now add the rice, stir lightly, cover and boil for 20–25 minutes.

When the rice is cooked, drain in a colander and serve. If serving later, re-heat in a steamer or microwave.

INGREDIENTS

COOKING TIME
20–25 minutes

2 bay leaves
A pinch of salt
2 tablespoons oil
225 g (8 oz) long-grain rice, washed and drained

PULLAO RICE
JEERA PULLAO

This is a basic rice pullao. You can add diced vegetables to make a vegetable pullao, or just one vegetable, such as peas, to make pea pullao.

INGREDIENTS

PREPARATION TIME
5 minutes
COOKING TIME
20–25 minutes

3 tablespoons ghee or oil
1 tablespoon cumin seeds
4 bay leaves
4 green cardamoms
225 g (8 oz) long-grain rice, washed and drained
Salt

Heat the oil or ghee in a saucepan with a tight-fitting lid. Add the cumin seeds, bay leaves and green cardamoms, and allow to brown. Now add the soaked and drained rice and stir-fry for 1 minute. Add salt to taste, then pour on 275 ml (9 fl oz) water and cover. Bring to the boil, reduce the heat and simmer for about 20 minutes until the rice is tender.

RICE WITH AUBERGINE
VANGI BHAT

An unusual, slightly sweet and nutty rice dish.

Process the chillies and ginger for a few seconds. Heat the oil or ghee in a saucepan and add the bay leaves, chillies, ginger, poppy seeds, cumin seeds and ground peanuts. Stir-fry until the spices are browned. Now add the sugar and let it caramelise slightly. Add the aubergine and cook for 1 minute. Then add the rice and stir-fry for 1–2 minutes. Pour in 275 ml (9 fl oz) water, bring to a fast boil, then reduce the heat, and leave to simmer until the rice is tender. Serve hot.

INGREDIENTS

PREPARATION TIME
10 minutes
COOKING TIME
20–25 minutes

2 green chillies
2.5 cm (1 in) fresh ginger,
peeled
4 tablespoons oil or ghee
2 bay leaves
2 tablespoons poppy seeds
1 tablespoon cumin seeds
4 tablespoons peanuts,
ground
1 tablespoon sugar
1 small aubergine, cut into
1 cm (¹/₂ in) cubes
225 g (8 oz) long-grain
rice, washed and drained

MARATHI TOMATO RICE
TAMATAR BHAT

This dish has a beautiful red colour with specks of green coriander. It looks wonderful displayed in a serving dish or bowl.

Heat the ghee in a saucepan and temper with the bay leaves and cardamom pods. Now add the onion and sauté until transparent. Add the ginger, garlic and chilli powder, fry for 1 minute, then add the rice. Gently stir-fry for 2–3 minutes, taking care not to break the rice grains. Pour in the tomato juice and simmer, covered, over a medium heat until nearly cooked. Add the tomatoes and continue cooking until the rice is tender. Serve garnished with the chopped fresh coriander.

INGREDIENTS

PREPARATION TIME
7 minutes
COOKING TIME
20–25 minutes

2 tablespoons ghee
2 bay leaves
2 green cardamom pods
1 large onion, peeled and chopped
1 tablespoon chopped fresh ginger
2 cloves garlic, crushed
¹/₂ tablespoon chilli powder
225 g (8 oz) long-grain rice, washed and drained
500 ml (18 fl oz) bottled tomato juice
2 medium tomatoes, skinned and quartered
1 tablespoon chopped fresh coriander

RICE WITH SPINACH
PALAK PILAU

A colourful rice dish – easy to cook and serve – which goes well with any curry. Though Basmati rice is the best type to use, one can substitute jasmine rice or brown rice.

De-stalk and wash the spinach, cut the leaves into strips and leave to drain in a colander.

Heat the ghee in a saucepan with a tight-fitting lid, and temper with the red chillies, bay leaves, peppercorns and coriander seeds. Add the rice and gently stir-fry for 2–3 minutes, taking care not to break the rice grains. Add 500 ml (18 fl oz) water, bring to the boil, then reduce the heat and cover.

Simmer until the rice is nearly cooked, add the spinach, mix lightly and continue cooking until the rice is tender. Serve hot.

INGREDIENTS

PREPARATION TIME
7 minutes plus 20 minutes
soaking time for rice
COOKING TIME
20–25 minutes

^{1}/$_2$ bunch spinach
1^1/$_2$ tablespoons ghee
2 dried red chillies, broken
into 2 halves
2 bay leaves
^{1}/$_2$ tablespoon black
peppercorns, crushed
^{1}/$_2$ tablespoon coriander
seeds, crushed
275 g (10 oz) Basmati
rice, washed, soaked for 20
minutes and drained

GOLDEN RICE WITH PEAS
MASALA BHAT

PREPARATION TIME
*10 minutes plus 20 minutes
soaking time*
COOKING TIME
20–25 minutes

*2 tablespoons oil or ghee
2–3 bay leaves
3–4 cloves
2 green cardamom pods
1 large onion, peeled and
chopped
225 g (8 oz) Basmati rice,
washed, soaked for 20
minutes and drained
1 tablespoon chilli powder
¹/₂ tablespoon ground
turmeric
2.5 cm (1 in) cinnamon
stick
A pinch of salt
100 g (4 oz) fresh or
frozen peas
2 tablespoons grated or
desiccated coconut
1 tablespoon chopped fresh
coriander*

A favourite dish of the Marathis, usually served on auspicious occasions with a curry or *dal*.

Heat the oil or ghee in a saucepan with a tight-fitting lid and temper with the bay leaves, cloves and cardamom pods. Add the onion and sauté until transparent.

Add the washed and drained rice, chilli powder, ground turmeric, cinnamon stick and salt. Gently stir-fry the rice for 2–3 minutes, taking care not to break the rice grains. Add the peas and then 500 ml (18 fl oz) water. Cook, covered, for about 20 minutes until the rice is tender and the liquid has been absorbed. Remove the whole spices and serve hot, garnished with the coconut and chopped fresh coriander.

AROMATIC RICE
VAGARE LA CHAWAL

The Parsis like to eat this rice dish on Sundays.

Heat the oil or ghee in a saucepan with a tight-fitting lid. Add the sliced onions and fry until dark brown but not burnt. Add the cinnamon, cardamom pods, cloves and cumin seeds and fry for 1 minute.

Now add the rice and stir-fry for 1 minute. Add salt to taste, then pour in 275 ml (9 fl oz) water, and cover. Bring to the boil, reduce the heat and simmer until the rice is tender and the liquid has been absorbed. Do not stir while cooking.

INGREDIENTS

PREPARATION TIME
8 minutes
COOKING TIME
20–25 minutes

3 tablespoons oil or ghee
2 large onions, peeled and sliced
1 cm (¹/₂ in) cinnamon stick
2 green cardamom pods
2 cloves
¹/₂ tablespoon cumin seeds
225 g (8 oz) rice, washed and drained
Salt

TAMIL RICE VERMICELLI
ARISI SEVAI

INGREDIENTS

PREPARATION TIME
6 minutes
COOKING TIME
10 minutes

250 g (9 oz) rice vermicelli
3 tablespoons oil or ghee
¹/₄ tablespoon mustard seeds
1 tablespoon split urd beans
4 whole dried red chillies
A few curry leaves
3 tablespoons grated or
desiccated coconut
2 tablespoons sesame seeds
A pinch of asafoetida
1 medium carrot, peeled
and grated
Salt
Lemon juice

R ice forms the staple diet of the South Indian Tamils and their cuisine includes many unusual rice derivations. Making rice vermicelli at home is rather time-consuming and tedious so many people nowadays buy commercially produced vermicelli which is equally good.

Boil the vermicelli in salted water, following the instructions on the packet. Then leave to drain.

Heat the oil or ghee in a saucepan and temper with the mustard seeds, split urd beans, red chillies, curry leaves, coconut, sesame seeds and asafoetida. Add the grated carrot and stir-fry for 1–2 minutes.

Now add the drained vermicelli, and season to taste with salt and lemon juice. Heat through and serve hot.

TIFFIN VERMICELLI

SEMIYA UPMA

Wheat vermicelli is normally used to make sweets in India – this is an unusual savoury combination. Italian vermicelli (which is more readily available than Indian) can be used instead. If you wish to add vegetables, sauté them before adding the vermicelli.

Heat the oil in a deep non-stick frying pan and temper with the mustard seeds, red chillies, split urd beans, curry leaves and cashew nuts. Add the vermicelli and stir-fry for 1–2 minutes.

Now add 750 ml (1¼ pints) boiling water and the salt. Bring back to the boil, then reduce the heat and leave to simmer, stirring occasionally, until the vermicelli is cooked. Add a little more water if necessary to complete the cooking.

Meanwhile process the ginger and green chillies for a few seconds and add to the vermicelli when it is cooked. Add lemon juice to taste, cook for a further minute, and serve.

INGREDIENTS

PREPARATION TIME
7 minutes
COOKING TIME
15 minutes

3 tablespoons oil
¹/₂ tablespoon mustard seeds
4 dried red chillies, broken into 2 halves
1 tablespoon split urd beans
A few curry leaves
3 tablespoons cashew nuts, broken
450 g (1 lb) vermicelli
A pinch of salt
2.5 cm (1 in) fresh ginger, peeled
2 green chillies
Lemon juice

FLAKY FRIED BREAD
PARATHAS

PREPARATION TIME
*20 minutes plus 15–20
minutes resting time for
dough*
COOKING TIME
3 minutes per paratha

*200 g (7 oz) fine
wholewheat flour
150 g (5 oz) plain white
flour
A pinch of salt
14 tablespoons oil or ghee*

Parathas are the Indian equivalent of flaky pastry except that they are far lighter and easier to make, and they are fried rather than baked. They can be made in all shapes and sizes, thick or thin. They can also be stuffed with all sorts of fillings (such as potato, cauliflower, mincemeat or peas) and are usually eaten with yoghurt, *raitas* or a light curry. Though making a good *paratha* requires a bit of practice, once you have mastered the art they are very simple to make.

————

Mix the wholewheat flour and plain flour in a bowl. If the wholewheat flour is grainy you may need to sieve it first. Add the salt, then pour 2 tablespoons oil or ghee into the flour, rubbing into the flour until you get a texture resembling breadcrumbs. Now add 175–200 ml (6–7 fl oz) water, using just enough water to form a soft dough. Knead the dough for 3–4 minutes, until it leaves the sides of the bowl and forms a single ball. Leave under a damp cloth to rest for 15–20 minutes.

Divide the dough into about 12 equal-sized balls. Dust with flour and roll each ball into a circle about 15 cm (6 in) in diameter. Spread with $^1/_4$ tablespoon oil or ghee and fold in half. Now spread with another $^1/_4$ tablespoon oil or ghee and fold in half again to form a triangle. Roll each *paratha* flat to make a 15 cm (6 in) triangle.

Heat $^1/_4$ tablespoon oil or ghee in a heavy-based frying pan and fry the first *paratha* for $^1/_2$–1 minute until it is dry. Turn over, spread with another $^1/_4$ tablespoon oil or ghee and fry until the *paratha* is golden brown with dark brown spots. Repeat with the others and serve hot. If they are to be served later, wrap them in a clean tea towel and seal wrap with kitchen foil.

SPICY POORIS
MASALA POORIS

Pooris (or *puris*) are very popular in Uttar Pradesh and Gujarat. They are served hot or cold and are usually eaten with curries, yoghurt or sweets. They are often sold in roadside stalls where one buys the *pooris* and gets the curry or yoghurt free. A tiny bit of spicy pickle goes very well with them.

Put the coriander, chillies, cumin seeds, kalonji seeds and peppercorns in a blender with 65 ml (2^1/$_2$ fl oz) water and blend to a smooth paste.

Mix the plain flour, wholewheat flour and salt together in a bowl. Then rub in the ghee until you get a texture resembling breadcrumbs. Mix in the blended spice mixture to make a soft dough, adding a little more water if required. Leave under a damp cloth to rest for 15–20 minutes.

Divide into 8–10 balls about the size of a lime and roll out into circles approximately 10 cm (4 in) in diameter, dusting with flour if necessary. Heat the oil to a fairly hot temperature in a *karai* or deep frying pan and drop in one *poori* at a time. Fry until the *pooris* puff up, turn with a slotted spoon and fry on the other side until golden brown. Drain on absorbent paper and serve hot.

INGREDIENTS

PREPARATION TIME
10 minutes plus 15–20 minutes resting time for dough
COOKING TIME
2 minutes per poori

1 bunch fresh coriander, washed
2 green chillies
^{1}/$_2$ tablespoon cumin seeds
^{1}/$_2$ tablespoon kalonji seeds
4 black peppercorns
100 g (4 oz) plain white flour
100 g (4 oz) fine wholewheat flour
^{1}/$_2$ tablespoon salt
2 tablespoons ghee
Oil to deep-fry

DIPS, CHUTNEYS AND PICKLES

Tangy, spicy chutneys and pickles – both fresh and preserved – form an integral part of Indian cuisine. Fresh pickles are usually consumed within a couple of days, whereas the preserved ones are eaten over several months. Preserved pickles are quite time-consuming and difficult to make, and it's often cheaper and easier to buy good-quality ready-made ones. For these reasons I have not included any preserved pickles in this chapter. Instead I have given several recipes for fresh pickles and chutneys which are quick and easy to make.

SPINACH AND YOGHURT RAITA
PALAK KA RAITA

An interesting variation on the usual *raitas*, this can be served as a side dish or dip. Use full-fat or low-fat yoghurt as you prefer.

De-stalk the spinach and cut the leaves into strips. Boil or steam in salted water for 1–2 minutes until tender, then drain in a colander. (Do not rinse with cold water.) When cool, lightly squeeze out the excess liquid. Then roughly chop the spinach and chill in the refrigerator.

Whisk the yoghurt, and stir in the cumin, black pepper and spinach. Season to taste with salt and serve garnished with chopped fresh mint.

INGREDIENTS

PREPARATION TIME
8 minutes plus chilling time for spinach

200 g (7 oz) fresh spinach
250 g (9 oz) plain yoghurt
1 tablespoon cumin seeds, roasted and ground
¹/₂ tablespoon black peppercorns, ground
Salt
1 tablespoon chopped fresh mint

POTATO AND YOGHURT DIP
ALOO PACHADI

A simple but deliciously tangy dip.

INGREDIENTS

PREPARATION TIME
10 minutes plus boiling and chilling time for potatoes
COOKING TIME
4 minutes

2.5 cm (1 in) fresh ginger, peeled
2 green chillies
200 ml (7 fl oz) plain yoghurt
1 tablespoon chopped fresh coriander
100 g (4 oz) potatoes, peeled, boiled and cut into 1 cm ($^1/_2$ in) cubes
1 tablespoon oil
$^1/_2$ tablespoon mustard seeds
A few curry leaves
1 tablespoon grated or desiccated coconut

Process the ginger and chillies for a few seconds. Then whisk the yoghurt with the ginger, chillies and $^1/_2$ tablespoon of chopped coriander. Add the diced boiled potatoes to the yoghurt, mix well and chill in the refrigerator.

Just before serving, heat the oil in a frying pan and temper with the mustard seeds, curry leaves and coconut. Stir this into the yoghurt and serve garnished with the remaining chopped fresh coriander.

MINT AND CORIANDER DIP
PUDINA AND DHANIYA
CHUTNEY

This dip is an ideal accompaniment to savoury starters such as fritters, and can also be served with a main meal.

Roughly chop the mint and coriander, wash in cold water and drain in a colander. Then blend to a paste with the green chillies, garlic, ginger, turmeric, salt and sugar, adding a little water if needed. Whisk the yoghurt and stir in the green spicy paste. If the dip is very thick you can thin it down with a little cold milk before serving.

INGREDIENTS

PREPARATION TIME
10 minutes minutes

2 tablespoons fresh mint
2 tablespoons fresh coriander
2 green chillies
1 clove garlic, peeled
1 cm (¹/₂ in) fresh ginger, peeled
¹/₂ tablespoon ground turmeric
A pinch of salt
¹/₄ tablespoon sugar
150 ml (5 fl oz) plain yoghurt

ONION RELISH
VENGAYA THUVAYAL

INGREDIENTS

PREPARATION TIME
8 minutes

2 large onions, roughly chopped
2 green chillies
2 dried red chillies
1 cm (¹/₂ in) fresh ginger, peeled
1 clove garlic
Salt
Lemon juice

This relish will usually keep in the refrigerator for 1–2 days.

Mix together the onions, chillies, ginger and garlic and blend to a purée, adding a very little water if necessary. Season to taste with salt and lemon juice, and serve chilled.

GARLIC AND CHILLI PICKLE
LASAN AUR MIRCHI KA ACHAR

An instant pickle made with vinegar. It is a nice variation from the regular oil-based Indian pickle. Make small quantities at a time, and store in an air-tight glass jar. Serve as a relish for main meals or snacks.

———

Heat the oil in a heavy-based saucepan and temper with the mustard seeds, fenugreek seeds and kalonji seeds. Add the green chillies, red chillies, garlic cloves, ginger, vinegar, sugar, salt and 65 ml (2½ fl oz) water. Bring to the boil, then reduce the heat and simmer for 2–3 minutes. When cool, store in the refrigerator in an air-tight container.

INGREDIENTS

PREPARATION TIME
15 minutes
COOKING TIME
8 minutes

2 tablespoons oil
½ tablespoon mustard seeds
¼ tablespoon fenugreek seeds
¼ tablespoon kalonji seeds
4 green chillies, chopped
4 dried red chillies, chopped
250 g (9 oz) garlic cloves, peeled and chopped
5 cm (2 in) fresh ginger, peeled and sliced
4 tablespoons white vinegar
1 tablespoon sugar
A pinch of salt

CHILLI AND GARLIC CHUTNEY
MILAGAI CHUTNEY

PREPARATION TIME
10–12 minutes

12 dried red chillies
6 cloves garlic, peeled
1 cm (¹/₂ in) fresh ginger,
peeled
¹/₂ tablespoon tamarind
pulp
1 tablespoon sugar
2 tablespoons oil
Salt

A tangy sweet chutney from the South, usually served with fried food like *vadas*, *pakoras* and *bondas*.

Dry roast the red chillies and garlic in a heavy-based pan. Remove and allow to cool, then mix with the ginger, tamarind, sugar and oil. Blend to a paste. (Do not add any water and ensure that the blender bowl is dry.) If the mixture is too dry to blend, add a little oil. Season to taste with salt. Store in an air-tight container.

MINT CHUTNEY
PUDINA CHUTNEY

The peanuts give this chutney a lovely crunchy texture.

Roughly chop the coriander, mint, green chillies, ginger and garlic. Wash and drain in a colander. Then blend to a paste with the remaining ingredients, adding a little water if necessary. Season to taste with salt and serve at room temperature or chilled with fritters or *pakoras*.

INGREDIENTS

PREPARATION TIME
10 minutes

*1 bunch fresh coriander
1 bunch fresh mint
4 green chillies
2.5 cm (1 in) fresh ginger,
peeled
4 cloves garlic, peeled
$^1/_2$ tablespoon cumin seeds
$^1/_2$ tablespoon ground
turmeric
1 tablespoon sugar
2 tablespoons roasted
peanuts
Salt*

DATE AND
TAMARIND CHUTNEY
KHAJUR AUR IMLI KE CHUTNEY

A deliciously sweet, sticky chutney.

INGREDIENTS

PREPARATION TIME
3 minutes
COOKING TIME
15–20 minutes

50g (2 oz) dates
25 g (1 oz) tamarind pulp
¹/₂ tablespoon fennel seeds
2 bay leaves
¹/₂ tablespoon ground cumin
2 tablespoons sugar
¹/₂ tablespoon ground ginger

Put all the ingredients in a heavy-based saucepan with 300 ml (10 fl oz) cold water. Stir to mix, bring to the boil, then reduce the heat and simmer for about 10 minutes until thick, stirring occasionally.

When the chutney thickens, remove from the heat, allow to cool, remove the bay leaves and chill. Store in an air-tight container. If the chutney is too thick, you can thin it down with a little cold water before serving.

MANGO SORBET (PAGE 119)

TOMATO AND CHILLI CHUTNEY
TAMATAR AUR MIRCHI CHUTNEY

This is a *very* quick and easy chutney – great to serve with fried titbits and snacks.

Mix together all the ingredients in a bowl and chill in the refrigerator. If the chutney is too thick, you can thin it down with a little cold water before serving.

INGREDIENTS

PREPARATION TIME
5 minutes

250 ml (8 fl oz) tomato ketchup
¹/₂ tablespoon chilli powder
¹/₂ tablespoon cumin seeds, roasted and ground
¹/₄ tablespoon black salt powder
¹/₂ tablespoon sugar (optional)

ICED LIME JUICE (*NIMBOO PANI*) PAGE 124, ICED TEA (*TANDA CHAI*) PAGE 122, AND SWEET YOGHURT DRINK (*MITHA LASSI*) PAGE 126

TOMATO CHUTNEY
TAMATAR CHUTNEY

A Bengali side dish which is usually made once a week and served chilled at the end of the meal.

PREPARATION TIME
5 minutes
COOKING TIME
20–25 minutes

2 tablespoons oil
1 tablespoon kalonji seeds
1 kg (2 lb) ripe tomatoes,
skinned and quartered
100 g (4 oz) sugar
2 tablespoons chopped fresh
ginger
1 tablespoon chilli powder
3 bay leaves
2 tablespoons raisins
A pinch of salt

Heat the oil in a heavy-based pan, temper with the kalonji seeds, and add all the remaining ingredients. Cook, uncovered, over a medium heat until the chutney is thick and glazed. Cool and store, covered, in a refrigerator.

106

APPLE CHUTNEY
SEB KI CHUTNEY

Most Indian families have their own methods of making all sorts of chutneys. I have used apples here but you can substitute any other fruit.

───────

Mix the apples with the salt in a bowl and leave for about 1 hour.

Now mix all the ingredients together in a stainless steel saucepan with 65 ml (2¹/₂ fl oz) water. Bring to the boil, then reduce the heat and leave to simmer, stirring frequently, for 20–25 minutes until the chutney thickens

Allow to cool, pour into a jar with a tight-fitting lid and store in the refrigerator. Remove the whole spices before serving.

INGREDIENTS

PREPARATION TIME
*8 minutes plus 1 hour
standing time for apples*
COOKING TIME
30 minutes

*6 medium cooking apples,
peeled, cored and diced
2 tablespoons salt
5 cm (2 in) cinnamon stick
2 whole dried red chillies
2 tablespoons chopped
fresh ginger
5 cloves
50 g (2 oz) sugar
4 green cardamom pods*

Coconut chutney
NARIAL KA CHUTNEY

INGREDIENTS

PREPARATION TIME
8 minutes

*225 g (8 oz) grated or
desiccated coconut
1 tablespoon mint leaves
1 tablespoon coriander
leaves
3 green chillies
1 tablespoon sugar
3 tablespoons lemon juice
¹/₄ tablespoon ground
turmeric
2.5 cm (1 in) fresh ginger,
peeled
3 cloves garlic
A pinch of salt*

Every region has its own version of coconut chutney. This one comes from South India.

Mix all the ingredients and blend to a paste, adding a little water if necessary. If you are using desiccated coconut, use coconut milk or yoghurt instead of water. (If you use yoghurt you may require a little more sugar.)

DESSERTS AND SWEETS

The recipes in this section are only a tiny fraction of literally thousands of Indian sweets. They are mostly made from milk or milk products and they tend to be sweeter than their Western equivalents. Most of these desserts can be made well in advance and will keep in the refrigerator for a couple of days.

You can use either granulated or caster sugar, but caster sugar will save time because it dissolves more quickly. Many of these recipes include ground cardamom. For speed and convenience you may wish to use bought ready-ground cardamom. However it is preferable to grind the cardamom seeds yourself in a coffee grinder, using seeds from green cardamom pods.

A word of warning about reducing milk for sweets: always use a pot which is absolutely clean and free from food stains or odours. You should also keep a special wooden spoon for stirring the milk.

CREAMY BREAD PUDDING
SHAHI TUKRA

This is a very popular dessert with Indian Muslims and it can be made in many different ways. In one variation you replace half the evaporated milk with 100 ml (3¹/₂ fl oz) fruit purée. Here is the basic recipe.

INGREDIENTS

PREPARATION TIME
6 minutes
COOKING TIME
15–20 minutes

200 ml (7 fl oz) sweetened condensed milk
200 ml (7 fl oz) evaporated milk
200 ml (7 fl oz) single cream
4 tablespoons ghee
6 thin slices white bread
¹/₄ tablespoon ground cardamom
1 tablespoon pistachio nuts, chopped
1 tablespoon slivered almonds, chopped

Mix the condensed milk, evaporated milk and cream in a saucepan and bring to the boil. Remove from the heat and keep warm.

Meanwhile, heat the ghee in a non-stick frying pan and fry the bread on both sides until it is golden and crisp.

Remove from the heat and cut each slice diagonally to make two triangles. Arrange in a serving dish and pour over the milk and cream mixture. Sprinkle over the ground cardamom and chopped nuts and leave to soak until ready to serve. Serve chilled.

RICE PUDDING
WITH NUTS AND RAISINS
KHEER

This dessert is usually made on auspicious occasions.

Put the milk in a heavy-based pan with the bay leaves and boil vigorously for 15–20 minutes. Reduce the heat, add the rice and simmer for another 20 minutes, stirring frequently, until the rice has cooked and the milk has thickened.

Now add the sugar and cook for a further 1–2 minutes. Remove the bay leaves. Stir in the ground cardamom, raisins and slivered almonds, remove from the heat and chill in individual bowls. Serve garnished with the chopped pistachio nuts.

INGREDIENTS

PREPARATION TIME
5 minutes
COOKING TIME
50 minutes

2.5 litres (4¹/₂ pints) milk
2 bay leaves
40 g (1¹/₂ oz) patna rice, washed and drained
100 g (4 oz) sugar or to taste
¹/₂ tablespoon ground cardamom
2 tablespoons raisins
2 tablespoons slivered almonds
2 tablespoons pistachio nuts, chopped

GOLDEN YOGHURT DESSERT
SHRIKAND

PREPARATION TIME
*7 minutes plus 2–2¹/₂ hours
hanging and setting time
minutes*

*1 litre (1³/₄ pints) plain
yoghurt
450 g (1 lb) sugar
2 tablespoons ground
cardamom
A few strands of saffron
1 tablespoon milk, slightly
warmed
2 tablespoons pistachio
nuts, chopped*

Although this recipe requires you to hang the yoghurt for about an hour beforehand, the actual preparation is very quick and easy.

Hang the yoghurt in a muslin cloth for about 1 hour to drain out the whey.

Remove and mix the drained yoghurt with the sugar and ground cardamom. Soak the saffron in the warmed milk for 2–3 minutes, then gently fold into the mixture. Pour into a serving dish, garnish with the chopped pistachio nuts and chill for 1–1¹/₂ hours. Serve chilled.

YOGHURT AND NUT SQUARES
DAHI KA MITHA

A nother drained yoghurt dessert. If you wish, you can make it more exotic by adding during the cooking a few strands of saffron soaked in milk.

Hang the yoghurt in a muslin cloth for about 1¹/₂ hours to drain out the whey.

Remove and put in a heavy-based saucepan. Add the sugar and cook over a low heat until the mixture is thick and leaves the sides of the pan. Mix in half the nuts and all the ground cardamom. Pour into a greased 20 cm (8 in) square baking tray and sprinkle the rest of the nuts over the top. When cool, cut into small squares and serve.

INGREDIENTS

PREPARATION TIME
7 minutes plus 1 ¹/₂ hours hanging time
COOKING TIME
15–20 minutes

500 ml (18 fl oz) thick plain yoghurt
450 g (1 lb) sugar
2 tablespoons slivered almonds
2 tablespoons pistachio nuts, crushed
¹/₂ tablespoon ground cardamom

ROSE-SCENTED
MILK CUSTARD
BASUNDI

PREPARATION TIME
5 minutes
COOKING TIME
30–40 minutes

1 litre (1³/₄ pints) milk
400 ml (14 fl oz)
sweetened condensed milk
1 drop of yellow food
colouring
A few drops of rose water
¹/₂ tablespoon ground
cardamom
2 tablespoons almonds,
chopped
2 tablespoons cashew nuts,
split
A few rose petals

This delicious dessert comes from Woodlands, a famous garden restaurant in Madras. It can be made well in advance and chilled.

Put the milk in a heavy-based saucepan over a high heat. Bring to the boil, then reduce the heat and simmer. Reduce by about two-thirds, then whisk in the condensed milk, food colouring, rose water, ground cardamom and half the nuts.

Spoon into individual bowls, sprinkle over the remaining nuts and garnish each portion with a rose petal. Serve chilled.

Mysore Fudge

MYSORE PAK

Mysore Pak is a dessert from the deep South, generally made during *Diwali*, the Festival of Light. It keeps for 2–3 days.

Heat 50 g (2 oz) ghee in a heavy-based pan, add the chickpea flour and fry until it turns brown and smells roasted.

Meanwhile put the sugar in a saucepan with 300 ml (10 fl oz) water and stir over a high heat for a few minutes until you have a frothy syrup. Now add about 25 g (1 oz) ghee to the syrup, reduce the heat and simmer for 1 minute. Add the fried chickpea flour, stir well and slowly add the remaining ghee.

Cook for a few minutes, stirring, until the mixture leaves the sides of the pan, add the ground cardamom and press into a shallow greased 20 cm (8 in) square baking tray. Cool, cut into squares and serve.

COOKING TIME
15–20 minutes

175g (6 oz) ghee
100 g (4 oz) chickpea flour
275 g (10 oz) sugar
1 tablespoon ground cardamom

COCONUT CANDY
TENGA BARFI

This popular candy keeps fairly well in an air-tight container and can be served after dinner with coffee.

COOKING TIME
15 minutes plus 30 minutes setting time

*270 g (10 oz) sugar
1 bay leaf
100 g (4 oz) desiccated coconut
4 tablespoons ghee
¹/₂ tablespoon ground cardamom*

Put the sugar in a small pan with 225 ml (8 fl oz) water and the bay leaf. Stir over a low heat until the sugar has dissolved, then bring to the boil and simmer for 3–4 minutes until you have a syrup.

Remove the bay leaf and add the coconut. Cook over a low heat, stirring occasionally, until the water evaporates. Add the ghee and fry until the mixture leaves the sides of the pan.

Stir in the ground cardamom and pour the mixture into a greased 25 cm × 20 cm (10 in × 8 in) baking tray using the back of a spatula to spread it out evenly. Leave to cool at room temperature, cut into small squares and serve.

COCONUT FRUIT SALAD
PHAL AUR NARIAL

Fresh fruits are the best way to end a meal. Here they are combined with dried fruit in a coconut sauce.

Peel and cut the fresh fruit into small pieces and set aside.

In a large bowl, mix together the coconut milk, ground cardamom, sugar and saffron. Whisk well and add half the dried fruit.

Just before serving, mix in the fresh fruit and arrange in a serving dish. Sprinkle over the remaining dried fruit and garnish with a few sprigs of mint.

INGREDIENTS

PREPARATION TIME
15–20 minutes

450 g (1 lb) mixed fresh fruit
250 ml (8 fl oz) coconut milk
1 tablespoon ground cardamom
2 tablespoons sugar
A few strands of saffron
2 tablespoons mixed dried fruit
A few sprigs of mint

CASHEW NUT FUDGE
KAJU BARFI

*B*arfi is widely used for devotional offerings. The basic fudge can be flavoured with other kinds of nuts such as pistachio, walnut, coconut or almond.

INGREDIENTS

COOKING TIME
15 minutes plus 1–1½ hours setting time

270 g (10 oz) sugar
2 tablespoons cashew nuts, broken
2 tablespoons unsalted butter
1 tablespoon plain white flour
100 g (4 oz) full cream powdered milk
½ tablespoon ground cardamom

Put the sugar in a small pan with 225 ml (8 fl oz) water. Stir over a low heat until the sugar has dissolved, then bring to the boil and simmer until a little of the syrup forms a thread when pulled. Dry roast the cashew nuts and keep aside.

Heat the butter in a heavy-based saucepan, add the flour and fry for 1–2 minutes. Add the powdered milk and stir. Now add the sugar syrup and reduce the heat to the minimum. Cook for 15–20 minutes, stirring occasionally, until the mixture leaves the sides of the pan.

Add half the cashew nuts and all the ground cardamom, then pour the mixture into a greased 25 cm × 20 cm (10 in × 8 in) baking tray. Sprinkle over the remaining nuts and leave to cool at room temperature for 1–1½ hours until set. Cut into small squares and serve.

MANGO SORBET

A frozen dessert is always popular on a hot summer day. This sorbet can be made well in advance and kept in the freezer. Mango pulp is available in tins. Alternatively you could peel and stone 2 small or 1¹/₂ large mangoes and purée in a blender.

Put the sugar in a small pan with 150 ml (5 fl oz) water. Stir over a low heat until the sugar has dissolved, then bring to the boil, and simmer for 3–4 minutes until you have a syrup. Remove from the heat and chill.

When the syrup is cold, add it to the mango pulp, together with the lime juice and ground cardamom. Mix well, pour into a mould and freeze for 30–40 minutes. Demould or scoop out into individual dishes for serving. Garnish with a few sprigs of mint.

INGREDIENTS

PREPARATION TIME
7 minutes plus chilling time for syrup
COOKING TIME
Depends on freezer and consistency required – usually 3–4 hours (for soft scoop)

150 g (5 oz) sugar
275 g (10 oz) mango pulp
Juice of 1 lime
¹/₃ tablespoon of ground cardamom
A few sprigs of mint

DRINKS AND SHERBETS

In this section I have included a couple of recipes for alcohol-based cocktails and a selection of cold drinks and sherbets.

Sherbets are extracts of herbs, spices and flowers blended in sugar syrup. In India there are shops which specialise in making and selling exotic-flavoured sherbets in concentrated form. They are normally diluted with chilled water, milk or yoghurt. The recipes I have chosen here are the ones which can be made with easily available ingredients. Always serve sherbets chilled and make them just before serving.

Bombay fizz

A very popular cocktail from the Harbour Bar at the Taj Mahal Hotel, Bombay.

———

Mix the mango juice and lemon juice in individual champagne flutes, then add the Champagne. You can vary the proportions according to whether you prefer a fruitier cocktail or one with more Champagne.

INGREDIENTS

PREPARATION TIME
1 minute

Mango juice
A squeeze of lemon juice
Champagne

ICED TEA

TANDA CHAI

PREPARATION TIME
5 minutes plus chilling time

Darjeeling tea
Sugar
Ice cubes
*A few slices of lemon or
lime*
A few fresh mint leaves

This colonial favourite has recently come back into fashion as a cocktail alternative.

Make a pot of tea with 750 ml (1¼ pints) water and add sugar to taste. Mix and allow to cool, removing the tea leaves once you have a strong brew. (If you leave them in the pot the tea will taste bitter.) Fill each highball glass one-third full of ice cubes, then pour over the iced tea and garnish with a slice of lemon or lime and a few mint leaves.

THE TEA RUNNER

A shot of dark rum is added to iced tea to make another cocktail.

Make a pot of iced tea and add a measure of dark rum (proportions may, of course, be varied!). Pour into highball glasses and decorate with mint leaves and slices of lime or lemon.

INGREDIENTS

PREPARATION TIME
*5 minutes plus chilling time
for tea*

*Iced tea (page 122)
Dark rum
A few fresh mint leaves
A few slices of lime or
lemon*

ICED LIME JUICE

NIMBOO PANI

INGREDIENTS

PREPARATION TIME
5 minutes

3 limes
Salt or *sugar*
A few fresh mint leaves
1 egg white, beaten
(optional)

The perfect drink for a very hot summer day, *nimboo pani* can be served either sweet or salted. Some people like to add a sprinkling of black pepper to enhance the flavour. You can also use this recipe for lemons, replacing 3 limes with 2 lemons.

Squeeze the limes into 1 litre (1³/₄ pints) of water and mix. Add salt or sugar to taste and whisk until dissolved. Shred a few mint leaves and add.

Serve chilled, garnished with a mint leaf and a slice of lime. If you wish, you could first dip the tops of the glasses in beaten egg white, then dip them in salt or caster sugar, to frost.

SPICED YOGHURT DRINK
MASALA LASSI

*M*asala lassi is a variation on plain salted *lassi*. This is a very popular drink at the Taj Mahal Hotel, New Delhi.

Blend or whisk the yoghurt, salt, roasted cumin powder and 750 ml (1¼ pints) water for 3–4 minutes. Now add the rest of the ingredients and mix well. Serve chilled.

INGREDIENTS

PREPARATION TIME
10 minutes

300 ml (10 fl oz) plain yoghurt
A pinch of salt
1 tablespoon cumin seeds, roasted and ground
1 green chilli, chopped
¹/₂ tablespoon chopped fresh ginger
1 tablespoon coriander leaves, chopped
1 tablespoon mint leaves, chopped
A few ice cubes

SWEET YOGHURT DRINK
MITHA LASSI

PREPARATION TIME
5 minutes

*300 ml (10 fl oz) plain
yoghurt
65 g (2¹/₂ oz) sugar
A few drops of rose water
¹/₄ tablespoon ground
cardamom
A few ice cubes*

This is probably the best known of the Indian sherbets.

Blend or whisk the yoghurt, sugar and 750 ml (1¹/₄ pints) water for 3–4 minutes. Add the rest of the ingredients and mix well. Serve chilled.

ALMOND YOGHURT DRINK
BADAMI SHERBET

During the summer in India, sherbets are often served in place of alcoholic beverages which are not always acceptable socially. *Badami sherbet* is an exotic non-alcoholic drink usually served on special occasions. A few strands of saffron can be added.

———

Blend the almonds, pistachio nuts and 250 ml (8 fl oz) water to a coarse paste. Add this to the milk, together with the ground cardamom and sugar to taste. Blend or whisk until the sugar dissolves. Add the ice cubes and serve chilled.

INGREDIENTS

PREPARATION TIME
7 minutes

2 tablespoons blanched almonds
2 tablespoons pistachio nuts
500 ml (18 fl oz) cold milk
1 teaspoon ground cardamom
Demerara sugar
A few ice cubes

MENUS

In India, courses are not separated as they are in the West. Nowadays all the food is usually laid out as a buffet from which one helps oneself. In my view this is a more casual and enjoyable way of eating and gives one a chance to appreciate the many different colours, aromas and flavours of Indian food.

The basic principle is that if you are serving rice then you should have at least one or two 'wet' dishes, whereas if you are serving bread, then you should serve drier dishes. Likewise, a good menu will also contrast sweet and sour, 'hot' and mild, and so on.

The following menus illustrate these principles and should help to give you ideas for your own combinations.

LIGHT MEAL

Pepper and Tamarind Consommé   *page 27*

KALA MIRCH AUR IMLI RASAM

Corn Kernels with Mixed Peppers   *page 80*

bhutte ke dane aur simla mirch

Tiffin Vermicelli   *page 91*

SEMIYA UPMA

Coconut Fruit Salad   *page 117*

PHAL AUR NARIAL

QUICK MEAL

Green Soup   *page 24*

CALDO VERDE

Mung Bean, Lettuce and Tomato Salad   *page 38*

MOONG DAL KOSUMALLI

Spicy Pooris   *page 93*

MASALA POORIS

COCKTAIL TITBITS

Cheese Chilli Toast   *page 78*

Crispy Fried Potato, Sago and Cheese Patties   *page 81*
SAGO ALOO VADAS

Fried Savoury Pastries   *page 76*
GAZA

SUNDAY BRUNCH

Channa Dal Fritters   *page 29*
CHANNA DAL BHAJIAS

Mushroom and Peas Korma   *page 45*
KHUMBI AUR MATTAR

Marathi Tomato Rice   *page 86*
TAMATAR BHAT

ROMANTIC MEAL

Potato Salad with Pomegranate   *page 40*
ALOO CHAMAN KI CHAT

Grilled Mushrooms   *page 77*

Courgettes Cooked in Pickling Spices   *page 51*
COURGETTE ACHARI

Tamil Rice Vermicelli   *page 90*
ARISI SEVAI

Golden Yoghurt Dessert   *page 112*
SHRIKAND

FORMAL ENTERTAINING

MENU 3

Crispy Sago Dumplings   *page 30*
SAGO BONDAS

Chutney-Coated Cauliflower   *page 49*
GOBI CHUTNEYWALI

Spicy Lentils with Vegetables   *page 57*
TARKARI DAL

Potatoes with Coconut and Cashews   *page 71*
ALOO PODIMAS

Mint Chutney   *page 101*
PUDINA CHUTNEY

Spicy Pooris   *page 93*
MASALA POORIS

Rose-Scented Milk Custard   *page 114*
BASUNDI

MENU 4

Pepper and Tamarind Consommé   *page 27*
KALA MIRCH AUR IMLI

Corn Kernels with Mixed Peppers   *page 80*
BHUTTE KE DANE AUR SIMLA MIRCH

Moghulai Potatoes   *page 63*
ALOO KA SALAN

Tangy Carrot Salad   *page 37*
GAJJAR KOSUMALLI

Flaky Fried Bread   *page 92*
PARATHAS

Yoghurt and Nut Squares   *page 113*
DAHI KA MITHA

MENU 5

Green Soup *page 24*
CALDO VERDE

Crispy Vegetable Rolls *page 75*

Cauliflower Gratin *page 79*

Potato Salad with Pomegranate *page 40*
ALOO CHAMAN KI CHAT

Marathi Tomato Rice *page 86*
TAMATAR BHAT

Mango Sorbet *page 119*

INDEX

Page numbers in *italic* refer to colour photographs